SOLUTION FOCUSED PRAC
SCHOOLS

Solution Focused Practice is a change-focused approach to enabling people of all ages to make progress in their lives by emphasising what is wanted in the future, amplifying successes and highlighting the capacities and skills available to support progress.

Grounded in the reality of the day-to-day challenges of school life, *Solution Focused Practice in Schools: 80 Ideas and Strategies* offers dynamic, practical, down-to-earth and jargon-free applications of the Solution Focused (SF) approach that can create energy and movement in even the toughest of situations.

From working with individuals to considering organisational developments, this book explores the SF approach using numerous examples and sample questions that can be adapted for any situation and whether the time available is long or short.

The reader will gain ideas about how to:

- move beyond 'don't know' responses in individual discussions with students to create dialogues where difference and change can occur
- invite classes into constructive conversations about building the classroom environment that brings out the best in students, whether there has been a concern or not
- address key issues such as confidence, motivation, resilience and dealing with set-backs
- build detail around potential and effective futures in coaching, consultations and meetings
- support the development of policies and procedures at an organisational level
- support solution-based conversations using play, role play, video and other creative techniques.

This book is an excellent resource for managers, teachers, SENCOs, mentors, counsellors, coaches, psychologists, social workers and all those who work in a supportive capacity in schools to promote the learning and well-being of both students and staff.

Yasmin Ajmal is a former primary teacher and educational psychologist. She is now self-employed as a Solution Focused coach, trainer and educational consultant.

Harvey Ratner is a founder member of BRIEF, established in 1989 to deliver therapy, coaching and training in the Solution Focused approach. He works as a therapist and coach at BRIEF and in schools.

'In this marvellous new book, Ajmal and Ratner teach us, in their own words, that "It is only the wearer of the shoe who knows where it is comfortable". Through providing the basics of the Solution Focused approach and using it with individuals, groups, staff members and teachers, the reader will gain true insight into how schools can work using Solution Focused Practice. The dialogues that are included offer rich, specific examples of how school counsellors, teachers and head teachers can engage and relate to students dealing with a variety of concerns. Educators who often wonder if they can make a difference with a troubled student need to read this book, which will finally provide them with ideas and strategies for asking questions that elicit teacher- and student-driven solutions, which are always the best kind!'

Linda Metcalf, author of *Counseling Toward Solutions* and Director of Graduate Counseling Programs and School Counseling at Texas Wesleyan University, USA

'This is an invaluable, inspiring and accessible guide for all teachers, from trainee to experienced, in responding effectively to the challenging situations encountered with individual children, groups and whole classes. The book is evidence-based and grounded in practice. It offers practical approaches that go beyond problem solving to enable pupils to recognise, own and sustain their "best selves". The process of co-constructing desired futures and achievable steps is illustrated through numerous case study examples. These studies highlight the impact of open questioning and scaffolded dialogue in building positive attitudes and relationships for learning and for life.'

Sue Ellis, Professional Tutor and Senior Teaching Fellow at UCL Institute of Education, UK

SOLUTION FOCUSED PRACTICE IN SCHOOLS

80 Ideas and Strategies

Yasmin Ajmal and Harvey Ratner

Routledge
Taylor & Francis Group

LONDON AND NEW YORK

First published 2020
by Routledge
2 Park Square, Milton Park, Abingdon, Oxon OX14 4RN

and by Routledge
52 Vanderbilt Avenue, New York, NY 10017

Routledge is an imprint of the Taylor & Francis Group, an informa business

British Library Cataloguing-in-Publication Data
A catalogue record for this book is available from the British Library

Library of Congress Cataloging-in-Publication Data
A catalog record has been requested for this book

ISBN: 978-1-138-64021-4 (hbk)
ISBN: 978-1-138-64022-1 (pbk)
ISBN: 978-1-315-63677-1 (ebk)

Typeset in Interstate
by Swales & Willis, Exeter, Devon, UK

CONTENTS

FOREWORDS

As a teacher with 32 years' experience, many of which have been as a head teacher, I am used to the daily pressures presented by running a school. Whilst most head teachers thrive in their role and indeed relish the challenge; working within such a high octane environment can feel similar to one of a Premiership football manager, where you are only as good as your latest result. The danger is that initiatives become driven by external agendas, leading you further away from key principles towards 'quick fixes' and pre-packaged solutions.

Five years ago, my own understanding of school improvement was turned upside down by Yasmin Ajmal, an education consultant with a background in educational psychology and solution focused (SF) practice. She was employed to support a challenging group of children in Year 5 who were posing a threat to our good reputation for high standards and excellent behaviour. Ultimately, her work would change both the way I approached my own role and the way I considered the role of others.

The initial work with the Year 5 class grew organically. It was bespoke to the children, the situation and the demands. Children were supported to think about their behaviour in terms of the skills they brought to the table rather than empty vessels needing to be filled with the skills of others. They were encouraged to see themselves within a process of progress through the use of scale questions. They were introduced to the language of SF and encouraged to ask questions. By applying scales and finding 'sparkling moments' children became forward thinkers and positive doers who actively sought their preferred outcomes. The work provided children with the tools (often referred to as arrow questions) vital for their input in shaping things. In doing so they became more committed to the outcomes.

One year later, with the same cohort moving to Year 6, the Student Ambassador project was born. The pupils themselves interviewed me about my vision and their role within it. This proved to be a challenge in itself; the students working together to probe my every comment, helping me to clarify in detail my overall vision of change. We had seemingly achieved the impossible; this initially challenging cohort was now driving school improvement for the benefit of all pupils.

However powerful for children, the wider legacy of the project was in how it demonstrated to staff the power of a SF approach to change. We had challenged their thinking and opened up new possibilities, leading staff at all levels to reconsider their aspirations for children. For example, lunchtime supervisors who had previously dismissed the potential for 'naughty children' to support lunchtime provision were now saying they could not now imagine their job without support from the very same pupils. Several key teachers became interested in the potential of SF practice, and so our journey continued with a wider agenda to improve shared working practices and support classroom practitioners to improve practice using this methodology as a key instrument for change.

The value of a SF approach is in terms of focus and clarity. Even in short meetings, it is possible to stretch the mind and imagination and finish a dialogue, having had a powerful discussion, giving you steps forward which lead towards positive change. The impact of leaving a discussion full of positive possibilities cannot be underestimated.

A SF approach helped our school to move forwards because the underlying principle was to put people in charge (staff and students) by asking questions and providing them with a framework within which they could think and evaluate their performance for themselves. An assumption of existing expertise built the self-esteem of the individuals involved in the change. Children and more junior staff were empowered because their views were now treated with importance. This motivated them to invest in the process of change as they were able to place themselves in the role of key drivers of success. Developments were non-threatening because, rather than relying on a deficit model, they always started with children and staff talking about the good things that were going well. The emphasis has been one of doing *with* rather than doing *to* children. This is the kind of culture that becomes infectious and will begin to change the ethos of a school.

I hope that, by reading this book and considering the case studies detailed within it, you will begin to recognise the power that a solution-based approach can give at every level of work in a school; whether it be in ways of working with senior leaders to implement change, ways that children can impact upon their own provision, or how lunchtime supervisors can become key drivers of school improvement. To work most effectively, one needs to understand the philosophy that backs up the SF approach and through many examples, this book illustrates the thinking underlying the questions that are asked, the techniques used and the impact of the ideas on practice.

A SF approach does not have to begin with grand plans; it can be started in simple ways and with a simple philosophy. Primarily one needs to build relationships within which people can grow. They need to find their own ways of being excellent by utilising what they can already do in order to become what they desire to be. The SF approach looks forwards not backwards; the direction of travel is to the future, not to the past. I now imagine what the children and staff 'can do', rather than dwell upon what they can't. The challenge is how to transform the pockets of outstanding that already exist to become the prevailing wind of change.

Chris Harrison
Head teacher, George Carey Church of England Primary School

Regent High is an inclusive school that seeks to offer those students who, at times, may need support through immediate or long-standing difficulties. For more than 20 years practitioners from BRIEF – Harvey Ratner, Yasmin Ajmal and Denise Yusuf – have offered our students a structured time to talk through their concerns using a Solution Focused approach. The impact of this intervention is significant in supporting the student in finding their own solutions. In addressing their issues themselves, students are empowered to draw on their own emotional resources and to meet challenges head on, which becomes a key life skill.

Sometimes, a handful of conversations over a few weeks will be enough to help the student to find a resolution to a problem, and for other students a longer-term approach is necessary. The Solution Focused approach is able to navigate these different needs to provide the most relevant and impactful experience for each student. The success of these conversations has meant that students are less likely to need any further referrals to other services.

It would be remiss of me not to mention the support provided to staff in dealing with a difficult professional or personal concern. The fact that the practitioners are based in school and are cognisant of the demands placed on school staff means that their concerns are explored in a timely and efficient manner. The space and time provided means that challenges are much less likely to become crises, which is essential for both the individual staff member but also the colleagues and students around them.

At Regent High School we recognise the privileged position we occupy by having Solution Focused support as part of the broader 'family' of the school. The positive impact of this support is significant: on the students and staff seeking support, on their friends and colleagues, on their families and on other services. It works in tandem with our ethos of creating a 'safe and positive learning environment' as it captures and holds students and staff when they are feeling at their most vulnerable, equipping them to successfully navigate the challenges they are facing. That there is now a guide for other settings to use and techniques that staff in schools across the country can apply is testament to the success of the Solution Focused approach, but also to the persistence of the book's authors in giving access to as many people as possible to this effective, impactful way of working.

Gary Moore
Head teacher, Regent High School

ABOUT THE AUTHORS

Yasmin is a former primary teacher and educational psychologist. She co-authored the first book on the use of the Solution Focused approach in UK schools (Rhodes & Ajmal 1995) and was co-editor of a further volume (Ajmal & Rees 2001) that demonstrated the wide applicability of the approach to all aspects of work in schools. She worked as trainer and therapist at BRIEF for 10 years and during that time also worked at an inner London secondary school as a coach for students and staff. Between 2008 and 2010 Yasmin worked in the education system in Zanzibar. After returning to the UK, she continued her career as an educational psychologist, working in secondary and primary schools with an additional focus on the early years. Yasmin is now self-employed as a Solution Focused coach, trainer and educational consultant (yasminajmal59@gmail.com).

Harvey is a founder member of BRIEF, an independent institute that delivers therapy, coaching and training exclusively in the Solution Focused approach (for details of courses and further information about current practice, please visit the BRIEF website www.brief.org.uk). He has worked as a coach and therapist at the same inner London school as Yasmin for more than 20 years. He is the co-author of 4 previous books on Solution Focused Practice, including *Solution Focused Brief Therapy: 100 Key Points and Techniques* (Ratner, George & Iveson 2012) and *Brief Coaching with Children and Young People* (Ratner & Yusuf 2015).

PREFACE

In this book, we discuss the key areas of application of the Solution Focused (SF) approach to support the day-to-day activity of teaching and learning in schools. Drawing upon our more than 20 years' experience of work in schools, and influenced by the popularity of the *100 Key Points* volume, the aim has been to highlight the main features of Solution Focused Practice (SFP) in a way that is simple, practical and efficient. In writing the book, we have kept in mind the needs of front-line staff. At the same time, the ideas explored will have a relevance for any practitioner involved in education, including those in a management, pastoral or therapeutic role. Each chapter is designed to illustrate how SF 'operates' alongside the underlying principles which guide practice and sample frameworks to support learning. In keeping with the practical objective of the book, numerous examples are drawn from our own practice and also from those of educational colleagues. These examples cover the full primary and secondary age ranges and attention is paid to the differences in style, techniques and communication to ensure adaptability across a breadth of needs and situations.

All chapters have been co-written by the two authors. We have not generally differentiated between Yasmin or Harvey in the numerous case examples, preferring to use the generic term 'practitioner' (P). Having said this, in the individual case discussion in Part 7, we are explicit as to who the worker is and there are other occasional specific references. Although each chapter is designed to stand alone, it is strongly recommended that every reader explore the Introduction to Solution Focused Practice in Part 1 as the background information and broad overview will provide a firm foundation for all those who are interested in building their skills and generating their own ideas.

A note about abbreviations: instead of repeatedly spelling out 'Solution Focus' we have used the initials 'SF' throughout and 'SFP' for 'Solution Focused Practice'.

ACKNOWLEDGEMENTS

We have both worked – and, in Harvey's case, continues to do so – in Regent High School (formerly South Camden Community School) in the London Borough of Camden, and we have enjoyed fruitful relationships with staff and students too numerous to mention. Yasmin would also like to acknowledge her productive years of work at George Carey Church of England Primary School and to thank Chris Harrison and all members of the George Carey staff who have given their time, thoughts and ideas to using a SF framework to support school initiatives. Particular thanks also to Richard Paul at Greatfields Secondary School for his interest in utilising a SF framework to support organisational developments. We would like to express our deepest appreciation of our closest colleagues in the Solution Focused world, Evan George, Chris Iveson and Denise Yusuf. Last but not least, our thanks go to our partners Martin and Tsila and the numerous friends and family members who have all so generously contributed their time, comments and support.

Part 1 Introduction to Solution Focused Practice

1. What is Solution Focused Practice (SFP)?

SFP is a change-focused approach that helps people find ways forward from difficult or challenging situations by focusing on what is wanted in the future and what is already working. For more than 30 years ideas first encountered in the world of therapy and counselling have been developed in creative and inspiring ways by education professionals. The interest in solutions rather than problems, the future rather than the past and people's resources rather than their deficits provides a structure which is aspirational and economical of time and resources. The adaptability of SFP is particularly apt for the school setting, offering a framework for developing constructive dialogues at an individual, group, class and organisational level. Within the context of diminishing budgets and over-full agendas, SF thinking offers a pragmatic approach to the discovery of solutions and new possibilities.

Many of our best ideas about tailoring SFP to the school environment have grown out of collaborative work with school staff. Our current practice and understanding has benefitted from the suggestions and pertinent questions they have posed. A constant feature of staff feedback on their use of SFP is the energy-giving effect of focusing on what is working and what is wanted, regardless of the task at hand.

Throughout the chapters there are numerous examples of how a SF approach can be incorporated into the busy day-to-day work in the classroom and the wider school context to support staff in cultivating the kind of school culture that they wish for the students and themselves. Readers will see a range of options for expanding or contracting discussions in relation to the time available including many examples of 5 minute conversation frameworks. At the heart of each chapter is the process of learning and exploring with students and staff the conditions that bring out the best in them in finding a way forward. It is never certain which questions will be useful until they have been asked, but it is hoped that examples from across the primary and secondary age ranges will boost the confidence of staff to explore and to experiment.

2. A brief background

The ideas contained within this book originated from the work of a creative group of researchers and therapists at the Brief Family Therapy Center (BFTC) in Milwaukee, established in 1977 by Steve de Shazer and Insoo Kim Berg. That the team included researchers was of immense importance to the development of the approach because it meant that from day one the team were checking whether the techniques they were employing were actually working. One of the most original of their innovations was the Miracle Question, which followed someone telling Kim Berg that her problem was so overwhelming that 'it would take a miracle to sort it out':

- Suppose that one night, while you are asleep, there was a miracle and this problem was solved. How would you know? What would be different? (de Shazer 1988: 5)

Rather than examining the problem, the aim of their work became to explore a person's life *after* the problem had been solved. Once described, it was then possible to look for those times they were already achieving this. Whatever was happening at these times were called 'exceptions' to the problem rule and could therefore form the basis of a solution. With this combination of *future focused* questions – how the person would know the problem had been solved and *exception* questions – what they were already doing about it – the team were able, by the mid-1980s, to announce that they had developed a new model. Instead of studying problem behaviour and trying to change it, they focused on solution behaviours and how to promote them. They subsequently devised the technique of a scale, from 0 or 1 to 10, as a way of elaborating the degree of progress that their clients had already made towards their goals.

Later developments

Since those pioneering days, the model of SFP has developed in different ways and BRIEF in London has been at the leading edge of these developments. For example, they have emphasised the importance of starting initial meetings with what has become known as the Best Hopes Question (Ratner et al. 2012):

- What are your best hopes from this meeting (discussion or piece of work)? How will you know our work together has been useful?

This leads to a modified version of the Miracle Question, known as the Tomorrow Question, to clarify in detail what the achievement of those hopes would look like, the person's 'preferred future' (Ratner et al. 2012: 93):

- Suppose tomorrow you found that you had achieved those hopes, what would be the first thing you'd notice yourself doing that would tell you that?

In keeping with this focus on the preferred outcome, 'exceptions' have been recast as 'instances': instances of the preferred future already happening (Ratner et al. op cit.).

3. Summary of practice

Current SFP would incorporate some or all of these elements:

- Finding out what is wanted – the difference or outcome – from the work to be done

- Exploring the 'preferred future' – the detail of what will be happening when the outcome has been achieved
- Identifying the instances of success – times the preferred future is already happening – and 'building on what is working'
- Denoting progress on a 0–10 or 1–10 scale – what has already been done to get to a certain point
- Noting possible signs of further progress towards the preferred outcome
- Summarising the work – often in the form of compliments.

4. Fundamental SF skills

The SF tradition has given us particular skills for change-focused conversations in schools.

Be pragmatic: focus on what people do

- What will 'getting on with your work' *look* like? What will you be doing?
- Suppose I was walking round the school, what would I *see and hear* that would be the evidence of student's showing respect towards each other and staff?

This emphasis on action does not mean feelings and emotions are ignored. Feelings and beliefs influence actions, and vice versa. When students talk about wanting to feel happier or more confident, we often say that other people can't see inside their heads and so will continue to ask:

- How will people know that you are happy?
- When you are more confident, what will they see you doing?

A common answer might be 'I'll be smiling'. However, 'smiling' is only one of the many criteria by which their happiness will become known to others. The intention is to build as much detail as possible. 'What else will tell them you're happy?' helps to bring obvious and less obvious ideas into view.

Adopt an interactional approach

This idea, originating from systems thinking, looks at how people in a situation influence each other. Thus, when people talk about changes happening, we can also enquire about how their actions will impact on others, and how the actions of others will then affect them. We might, for example, ask a student to think about the following sequence:

- What their fellow students will notice differently about them when things are going better ...
- How they will know the others have noticed ...
- And then what effect *that* will have on them.

Consider the following conversation with a 9-year-old boy called Freddie whose behaviour is causing concern at both home and school. Freddie is talking about having a good day in school. The practitioner asks Freddie to think about what this will look like. Freddie thought the first thing his teacher would notice is that he would say 'good morning' to her in the corridor before school started.

Practitioner:	It's Monday morning and you see Miss Harris and you go 'Good morning Miss Harris'. What's she going to do when you say that?
Freddie:	She's going to say, 'Good morning' back.
Practitioner:	Will she?
Freddie:	Yeah.
Practitioner:	Will she be surprised?
Freddie:	Yeah.
Practitioner:	Would she be pleased?

SF questions are by and large open questions that help people to discover things about themselves. These are questions that can't be answered with a single word (like 'yes' or 'no') so that the answer can be used to feed back into the ongoing conversation. However, as can be seen in this extract, at times a closed question can be used to lead into an opening up question.

Freddie:	Yeah.
Practitioner:	How would you know? You know your teacher well now don't you? How would you know that she's pleased?
Freddie:	'Cos she has a voice when she's angry, when she's upset, when she's happy.
Practitioner:	Ok. So she's got different voices, yeah .... And so what voice will she use on Monday?
Freddie:	Well her face would light up.
Practitioner:	Oh! How nice. Would you like that if it did?
Freddie:	She does it sometimes.
Practitioner:	Does she? She's done it sometimes to you?
Freddie:	Yeah. And other children.
Practitioner:	And other children. And do you like it when she does that? What does it make you feel like when she does that?
Freddie:	Happy.

Seek descriptions rather than single answers

We aim for a rich picture of what change will look like. When a student says, 'I'll be better behaved in class', we can't know for sure what they mean by that, although they probably think it's the 'right' answer to give. If this in itself was sufficient to drive change, then that would be fine, but 'ready answers' rarely do that. Each descriptive detail elicited offers a possibility of a route through to change and difference. The more routes there are the greater the chance that something different will happen.

Consider the following example with a Year 9 student talking about his Science lesson.

Mentor:	You say it would be better for you to behave in class. What difference would that make?
Student:	Not sure. I don't know. I wouldn't be getting into trouble with the teacher.
Mentor:	What would be happening instead?
Student:	She'd leave me alone! She is always on about things. Even when it isn't me. She just picks on me.
Mentor:	Ok. And how would that be good for you, if your teacher was leaving you alone?
Student:	I don't know.
Mentor:	What do you think?
Student:	Mmm. Well if she left me alone, I could just get on with my things.
Mentor:	How would your teacher know you were getting on with your things?
Student:	What do you mean?
Mentor:	If you were getting on with your things, what would the teacher see?
Student:	I'd have my books out.
Mentor:	Would that be different?
Student:	Suppose so. Usually they are in my bag.
Mentor:	Would your teacher like that?
Student:	I guess.
Mentor:	How would you know that she liked seeing you get your books out?
Student:	She'd probably say something.
Mentor:	What else would be a sign of 'getting on with things'?

Building incremental and detailed descriptions can help to place a student in a future that would work better for them. In doing so, it can also create the idea that they are on a path to what feels like an achievable reality.

5. Solution building is not the same as problem solving

How we position ourselves with regard to 'solving problems' can make a difference to the type of questions we ask. SFP seeks to ask questions that enable people to build their own solutions rather than focusing on the problem or guiding them towards what we think would be useful. Take a student who is finding it difficult to get up in the morning. The more open question 'suppose tomorrow you managed to get up on time, what would be different?'- as opposed to the more closed question 'do you have an alarm clock you can use?'- both establishes the focus on getting up and encourages the student to build a description within which useful ideas may emerge. They might talk about setting a repeat alarm or something different - one student suggested a friend would call him each morning! Although it might seem quicker to tell people what to do, research shows that if people use their own expertise about what fits with them, they are both more motivated to do those things and more likely to sustain them.

6. Key SF questions

SF questions can be structured to accommodate any length of conversation, whether in the classroom, corridor or meeting room. Here are examples of short conversation structures:

2 minute conversation framework

> Think of something you would like to be better at.
> How would it be good for you if things improved in this way?
> What have you already done that has been useful?
> What would be the first small signs of progress?
> How would this show?
> What else will you be noticing?

5 minute conversation framework

> How will you know this conversation has been useful?
> And if that were to happen, what difference would it make? (What else? What other differences would you notice?)
> What would be the first signs of things improving? What else would you and others notice?
> What would be the smallest signs that things are moving in the right direction? What else? What else?

Questions that help to oil the wheels

Five of the most useful questions that can ease the flow of SF conversations are:

1.   The Great Instead

It is common for people (students and others) to answer questions in terms of what they *won't* do or *didn't* do. 'I won't be hearing bad news all the time from school' 'I didn't hit Billy that time even though he annoyed me'. It is extremely useful to remember 'The Great Instead' (Ratner et al. 2012: 70). 'What will you be hearing about *instead*?' 'What did you do *instead* of hitting Billy?'

2.   Difference questions

Sometimes it can be useful to further explore the outcome that a particular idea or action might lead to: 'If you aren't hearing bad news all the time, what difference will that make?' 'When you managed not to react to Billy, were you pleased about that? What difference did it make to you? What difference did it make to the class?'

3.   Other person perspective questions

As has already been discussed, asking about what significant others will notice or have noticed is a valuable source of SF questions.

4.   Keep it small

The smaller and more concrete the descriptive detail, the easier it is to see and do: 'What will be the smallest signs of things improving? And what will be the first signs of that?'

5.   'What else?'

It has been said that 'What else?' is the most commonly asked SF question of all. The more details that emerge, the more options for change become available. This sometimes needs prompting: 'So you won't be hearing bad news all the time from school. What else will be happening when things are going better?' 'So that was one difference it made not reacting to Billy. What else?'

7. Scales: denoting the progress already made

A 0-10 scale provides an accessible conversational framework (Ratner, forthcoming) which can invite consideration of all the key elements of a SF approach:

- The 10 represents success in whatever someone wants to achieve.
- Their current position can help us to reflect on how far they have come *and* to begin exploring all the useful behaviours and resources that have contributed to this.
- Looking at what will be different when they are +1 on the scale can help to identify small signs of progress in the right direction.

Motivation and interest in a scale is aligned to how closely the 10 on the scale represents the desired future of the person or people we are working with. It will be of little use constructing a scale about rugby skills with someone who has little interest in watching, let alone playing, the game. The flexibility of movement up and down a scale can encourage a greater sense of control and efficacy within the ups and downs which are a normal and ever-present feature of life. There are an enormous number of scales that are relevant to the school's context, some of which will be explored in detail throughout the book, such as working well together, being focused, temper control, having good friendships and 'the school we want to be'.

Example of a broad scale framework

> On a scale of 0-10, where 10 is all that you've said about the 'best version' and 0 is the worst it's been, where are you now? How come? What tells you that? What have you done that has been helpful?
>
> What tells others that you're there and not at 0? Which things do you think they will have been most pleased about?
>
> How will you know you've reached +1? What will you and others notice? What else?

A few tips when using scales

- The 10 must be the presence of something and not the absence of a problem.
- The 0 is often referred to in broad terms such as 'the worst things have been'. The intention is to encourage a number higher than the 0, as a 0 can often block thinking around the things that have been useful or that someone has been doing.
- Even so, a 0 position can still be followed up with an eye to locating even small behaviours that have, or can be, helpful. 'How are you coping or managing?' can make available useful strategies as well as a question like 'What are you doing to stop things being even worse?' 'Given how tough things are, how will you know that this conversation has been useful?' acknowledges that the person is there for a reason and it might be pertinent to spend some more time solidifying this.
- Accept the number someone gives. This is *their* number rather than an objective assessment. There is often the temptation to be encouraging about numbers, particularly with students who place themselves low down. Rather than telling them that they are doing well or reminding them of things that they have been doing that would seem to contradict the number, there are two useful strands of enquiry. The first is to acknowledge that they would like things to be better and then find out how they have managed to stop things going even lower. Alternatively, we can ask students about the times when things have been higher and then find out all that was different at those times. Either enquiry might help bring into focus useful, yet temporarily forgotten, resources and behaviours.
- The most important point about the use of scale questions is the access it gives to the instances of success already present, and so it is helpful to slow down the process and resist the urge to move on quickly to the process of moving up the scale.
- When looking for signs of progress, of +1, as a preference we are seeking *descriptions* rather than goal-oriented plans. There is a wealth of difference between a question like 'If you were to be at +1, what would be different then?' and 'What are you going to do to reach +1?' The former is less challenging of the student, and doesn't commit them to a plan of action, as in the second case. Abdul a Year 9 student was in trouble for fighting. His current number on a 'keeping out of trouble' scale was a 3. He found it difficult to answer the question 'What will it take for you to move to a 4?' However, when asked a reshaped version, 'How will you know when things are at a 4?' he talked

about being 'less visible', which would include sitting down with a couple of friends so he was not in a large group and avoiding the hall at lunchtime. This is not to say that problem-solving questions such as 'What will it take …?' 'What are you going to do …?' are wrong, simply that it is often easier to answer in the realm of description rather than under the pressure of action. Concern about committing yourself to something you are not yet sure you want to do, may keep the best and most creative ideas dormant.

- The scale is usually offered in the numerical way described above, but there are as many types of scales as there are young people. The creativity of staff in schools has spawned numerous examples utilising all the senses, such as a student's favourite to least favourite foods; using pictures of faces ranging from sad to happy or from small smiling faces to large ones; physical scales drawn on the floor or represented by a line of chairs.

8. Dealing with 'don't know'

Staff routinely encounter students of any age who seem to answer most if not all questions with a shrug and a 'don't know'. Whilst it is not always easy to resist the urge to step in and provide an answer, here are some options we can hold in mind.

- *Wait*: 'I don't know' can be a habitual answer and if we wait, then we are emphasising the conversational rule of turn-taking where a non-response is a clue to the student that it is still their turn.
- *Return to the original question with a slight change in emphasis*: 'What do you *think* might be a sign that things are improving?' Or a more playful 'Have a guess'.
- *Acknowledge that this is a hard question and give an explanation of the reason behind it*: 'These are not always easy questions to answer and it is really important that I understand what things would look like from your point of view'.
- *Pave the way*: 'Can I ask you a hard question?' places emphasis on the question rather than the student for the difficulty in finding an answer. 'Can I have another go?' places emphasis on us to find a useful and understandable question. This is especially helpful with younger children.
- *Use the perspective of others*: 'What do you think your best friend (or teacher, or parent) would say they'd be happy to see you doing?'

9. Adapting SFP to work in schools

One to one work with students

In some situations it is possible to start a conversation with 'What are your best hopes from our talking together?' or 'How will you know this has been useful?' However, in most day-to-day work students and teachers are working towards the same broad preferred outcomes, such as a happy student working to the best of their ability in the environment of a happy class and school. What we want to discover is the student's own ideas of what 'being happy' is, in a way that is right for them and for the school.

Returning to Freddie, the 9-year-old boy who would be saying hello to his teacher Miss Harris, what he wanted was to have a good day, be happy and get on with people. The conversation tracked through what this would look like as he entered the classroom.

Practitioner:	So, the bell has gone and that says it's the beginning of the day. As you are going into your classroom, what would Miss Harris see you do that would make her go 'Wow'?
Freddie:	Put my bag away, put my coat away, put my homework in the homework box, sit up straight.
Practitioner:	Gosh – do all those things at the same time or which would you do first?
Freddie:	I'll put my bag and coat away, put my homework in the homework box and sit up straight.
Practitioner:	Sitting down on the mat and sit up straight?
Freddie:	I'd sit up straight on the chairs.
Practitioner:	On the chairs. Are you sitting up straight now or would you be doing it in a different way?
Freddie:	In a different way.
Practitioner:	Show me how you are going to sit up.

(Freddie sits up in his chair with his arms folded almost around his neck and looks at me)

Practitioner:	Oh wow. And what does that tell her, if you are sitting up straight like that? What would that tell your teacher?
Freddie:	That I'm paying attention to her.
Practitioner:	Ok. And would that be good? Would she like that?
Freddie:	Yeah.
Practitioner:	Have you done that before, gone into class like that?
Freddie:	No.
Practitioner:	Wow, so that would be a real first. Would Miss Harris be fainting on the floor by this stage? What would she be doing when she sees you doing all those things?
Freddie:	She would probably drop down on the platform!
Practitioner:	You'd have to go and fan her, wouldn't you?!

(Freddie giggles).

The rest of the discussion tracks Freddie's day into the school assembly and outside at playtime. Freddie was also encouraged to build details through the eyes of others: 'What will the head teacher see as you walk into assembly that will tell her this is a good day when you are happy and things are going well?' As each layer of detail was added, so Freddie's image of himself as someone who had ideas about how to make his day go better grew. The desire is not to set targets or goals. The purpose is to set a scene of possibilities: to set the ball rolling in the right direction where Freddie can be helped to find his own pathway to a more successful and ultimately rewarding time in school. A couple of weeks later Freddie returned clutching a certificate celebrating a good day.

Of course, the description of what *might* be does not mean that it *will* be. For example, a little earlier in the chapter Freddie mentioned his teacher's face 'lighting up'. What would happen if Miss Harris has had a bad journey in the morning and is not capable of having a face that lights up before her morning coffee? The reason for including a number of descriptions is that it allows for more than one opportunity. 'Who else will you see first thing in the morning?' 'What else will Miss Harris be noticing that makes her face light up?' or 'What else will you be doing on this good day?' – all these questions provide a wide choice so that expectation or success does not reside in one detail.

This was a first meeting with Freddie. Here is an example from a *follow up* conversation, where the aim is to 'build on what works':

Claire, a Year 7 student, had recently improved her attendance in school but was struggling to stay in many of her lessons. Starting from the basis of having successfully got herself back into school, which had been hard, the practitioner and Claire sat together with a large sheet of paper and began to list all her 'finding a way through challenges' skills. When this was finished, she looked at the list and said: 'I can't believe I have been doing all those things'. It provided a base of competencies from which it was now possible to ask:

- Which of these 'finding a way through challenges' skills are already present in your lessons?
- Which of these other 'finding a way through challenges' skills can your classmates and teachers look forward to finding out about?

When things are tough, 'How have you managed to keep things going in the face of such difficulties?' is not intended as an isolated question but as an entry point into a sequence – a sequence in which it will be important to keep in mind the 'toughness' and also maintain a curiosity about *how* the person persisted, despite all that was happening. This should not in any way be an attempt to show that things are not as bad as they seem. At the same time, never underestimate the importance, in challenging times, of our belief and hope in the people with whom we are working and the possibility of change.

5 minute conversation prompts for building on what works

> What is the closest things have come to (insert what is wanted: for example, things being more settled)?
> What was happening at this time?
> What were you most pleased to notice?
> How did you get those things to happen?
> What have you learnt from this and how will you know this is becoming even more useful now?

Everyday situations

A deputy head teacher passed a Year 4 student, Moneya, who was sitting outside a classroom. Moneya told her that she was waiting for her class teacher to say that she could go back in.

The deputy head asked Moneya: 'How will your teacher know that you are ready to go back in?'

She could equally have asked:

- What will your teacher notice when you go back in that would tell him you are ready?
- What will you be pleased to notice about yourself when you go back in?

There is no one right question. What binds all of these questions together is 'being ready to go back into the classroom' and focusing on actions that could support this. In this case Moneya said that she would be quiet and go and sit down. 'What other good things will your teacher see that will tell him that you are ready to go back into the classroom?' helps to bring a number of possible behaviours into the range of vision of the student, any one of which might make a difference. Utilising what the student is currently doing can also help bring a clarity to what a particular behaviour would look like: 'Will you be talking to your teacher like you are doing with me now, or will you be doing it in a different way?' Moneya said she would be doing this in the same way.

Moneya then commented that she wanted to get a good point on the behaviour system in the class. So the deputy head asked: 'What other good things will your teacher be seeing to tell him that you are on the way to a good behaviour point?' 'On the way' says that it is possible, whilst at the same time helping the student to think in terms of behaviour over time rather than success residing in a one-off action.

Work in the classroom

The staff in a Year 3 class helped the children to build a list of 20 things that showed what 'good learning' looked like in their class. By showing and describing what they had already done, the children were demonstrating that these were things that they could already do but might not have been aware of until they were noticed and named. Daily 5 minute observations were introduced: an adult wrote down what two student observers noticed was happening in the class and the notes were added to the list until there was an enormous record of over 100 things on the wall at the front of the class. The students were very proud of their list. It was a huge visual testament to their skills as learners. They were keen to bring it to the attention of any visitor to the classroom, which was a great clue to the visitor about what they could look out for and comment on.

Conversations with staff

A head teacher wanted to talk about a troubled 6-year-old boy who had stretched even her creativity and persistence. She wanted help in how to manage him but only had a couple of minutes prior to a meeting. With the opportunity to ask only a couple of questions, it is important to think about those questions which will most support potential difference or change.

Practitioner:	Sounds like you have put a lot of thought and effort into this. Given that you only have a few minutes now, can I ask you some questions?
Head Teacher:	Yes.
Practitioner:	What would be the first small sign of progress?
Head Teacher:	Well, if I could get our relationship back onto an even keel more quickly after I have had to tell him off. There are times I have to do this, when his behaviour is unacceptable and it is important to the other children and his teacher that I step in.
Practitioner:	Ok. So, what would be the first signs of getting your relationship back on an even keel more quickly?
Head Teacher:	That we could have a conversation together or do something together.
Practitioner:	What difference would that make?
Head Teacher:	Well he likes helping out with things and it is a good chance for us to have a chat. He often tells me things.
Practitioner:	What would he notice about you after the 'telling off' that would tell him you are ready for chats and help?
Head Teacher:	I suppose I'd smile at him. (*Pause*) I don't know. I smile anyway! (*Pause*) Maybe make a point of asking for help. Or maybe that we have regular helping times that are there whatever he has done. (*Pause*) So it is a consistency. That's it. A routine. Must go!

10. Summary of SFP in schools

SFP is:

> Positive: in the sense of being focused on what is wanted in future rather than what is not wanted ('What will you do *instead*?') and on what people have been able to do well rather than not.
>
> Future focused: conveying a belief and hope in future change through our questions.
>
> Empowering: enabling students and others to build a sense of ownership and also to help us notice our own successes as practitioners.
>
> Skills-based: holding the belief that people have the skills they need to build the future that they want.
>
> Interested in the actions behind the actions: not just saying 'Well done!' but 'Well done! How did you do that?'
>
> Time effective: whether we can talk for 2 or 22 minutes, there is time for a useful conversation.

> Generic: being *Solution* Focused means the approach can be used in the widest range of situations whether at an individual, class or organisational level.
> Context based: looking at what supports this student, this class or this school to do well in this situation.
> Complimentary: teachers need no reminding about the value of praising students and colleagues. The approach lends itself easily to finding good things to highlight.

11. Research and literature on SFP

It works!

Right from the start SFP has asked 'Does this work?' and striven to conduct research into its efficacy. Today there is a considerable evidence base for SFP (Franklin et al. 2012; Gingerich and Petersen 2013; Kelly et al. 2017) and a growing body of research within that evidence base that shows its effectiveness in the field of education. In Scotland, there has been impressive research carried out into the effectiveness of the WOWW approach (Brown et al. 2012; Lloyd et al. 2012). WOWW stands for 'Working on What Works' (Berg and Shilts 2005; Kelly et al. 2017; Ratner et al. 2012; Shilts 2013). The essence of the approach is one of observation: noticing everything and anything that goes well in lessons and feeding this back to students.

Literature

There has been much that has been written on the application of the approach in school contexts. We have mentioned Berg and Shilts (2005), Shilts (2013) and Kelly et al. (2017). Internationally there is also Metcalf (2003, 2009), Mahlberg and Sjoblom (2004) and Franklin et al. (2018). In the UK, there have been books by Rhodes and Ajmal (1995), Ajmal and Rees (an edited volume of work by several practitioners, 2001), Young (2009) and James (2016). In addition, there are articles and chapters in many places including work by ourselves, such as Ratner (2003), Ajmal (2006), Ratner et al. (2012) and Ratner and Yusuf (2015). New material is appearing all the time and among the places to look is *Solution News*, the on-line magazine of the United Kingdom Association for Solution Focused Practice and the international *Journal of Solution Focused Brief Therapy*.

12. How to get going … and how to keep going

Getting going

It's all about practice, but where to start?

When I (YA) first came across the SF approach I initially experimented with the questions in more straightforward conversations to help my competence and understanding. I figured that the student who says 'don't know' to everything asked of them would give me little opportunity to explore the potential of the SF ideas I was most interested in! I would have a go at one or two questions and then reflect on the responses – what had worked and what I might do differently next time. In this way, I gradually built up my confidence and repertoire of questions.

Keeping going

When stuck, I would also sometimes take a step back and give myself time to think:

- What was I pleased to notice about what I did even though it was tough going? It is always good to proceed from a position of strength.
- Has the person I am talking with shown any interest, however small, in any parts of the conversation? How could this be built on?

A few rules of thumb

- Can I see it? Am I focused on what someone *will* be doing, rather than won't be doing? Perhaps I need to remember The Great Instead (Ratner et al. op cit.). What will you be doing instead? What did you do instead?
- For every detail that emerges, think of how to embed it in the everyday classroom or school life. What will that look like at the beginning of the lesson? How will it show?
- Remember to use the perspective of others: What will the class notice you doing? What do you think I saw you doing that impressed me?
- Remember the *difference* questions: What difference will that make? What difference did it make?
- As much as possible, draw on the words the other is using.
- Ask one more 'What else?' than you feel comfortable asking. There is always more to be found.

Building sequences

Perhaps the hardest thing is to build a *sequence*. Although a SF conversation mainly consists of us asking questions and students, parents or staff answering, it is not an interrogation and we are not seeking information. As has been described already, we fold what the person has said back into our next question. Here is an example of what we mean:

A conversational sequence with a student

I want not to get distracted.	
	If you are not getting distracted, what will you be doing instead?
I will be focusing.	
	What would be a sign of this focus?
I will be looking at my book and reading the questions.	
	So, you will be looking at your book and reading the questions. What else would be a sign of you focusing?
Paying more attention to what the teacher is saying.	
	How will your teacher know that you are paying attention to what they are saying?
I might answer a question or ask a question.	

Looking back from now, this is the advice I would give myself

- Trust that you can ask one more question.
- Trust that if you build a conversation around outcomes something useful will emerge.
- Take one question at a time, that way you will not be overwhelmed by your own capacity and the situation.
- Don't give up on questions. If someone can't immediately answer try repeating, rephrasing or clarifying.

References

Ajmal, Y. (2006) Solution Focused Mediation in Schools. *Solution News* 2 (1): 3-6.

Ajmal, Y. and Rees, I. (Eds.) (2001) *Solutions in Schools*. London: BT Press.

Berg, I.K. and Shilts, L. (2005) Keeping the Solutions inside the Classroom. *ASCA School Counsellor* July/August.

Brown, E., Powell, E. and Clark, A. (2012) Working on What Works: Working with Teachers to Improve Classroom Behaviour and Relationships. *Educational Psychology in Practice* 28 (1): 19-30.

de Shazer, S. (1988) *Clues: Investigating Solutions in Brief Therapy*. New York: Norton.

Franklin, C., Streeter, C.L., Webb, L. and Guz, S. (2018) *Solution Focused Therapy in Alternative Schools: Ensuring Student Success and Preventing Dropout*. London: Routledge.

Franklin, C., Trepper, T.S., Gingerich, W.J. and McCollum, E.E. (Eds.) (2012) *Solution-Focused Brief Therapy: A Handbook of Evidence-Based Practice*. New York: Oxford.

Gingerich, W.J. and Petersen, L.T. (2013) Effectiveness of Solution-Focused Brief Therapy: A Systematic Qualitative Review of Controlled Outcome Studies. *Research on Social Work Practice* 23 (3): 266-283.

James, G. (2016) *Transforming Behaviour in the Classroom: A Solution-Focused Guide for New Teachers*. London: Sage.

Kelly, M., Kim, J. and Franklin, C. (2nd edition, 2017) *Solution Focused Brief Therapy in Schools: A 360-Degree View of Research & Practice*. Oxford: Oxford Univ Press.

Lloyd, C., Bruce, S. and Mackintosh, K. (2012) Working on What Works: Enhancing Relationships in the Classroom and Improving Teacher Confidence. *Educational Psychology in Practice* 28 (3): 1-16.

Mahlberg, K. and Sjoblom, M. (2004) *Solution Focused Education*. www.fkce.se.

Metcalf, L. (2nd edition, 2003) *Teaching Toward Solutions: A Solution Focused Guide to Improving Student Behaviour, Grades, Parental Support and Staff Morale*. Arlington, Texas: Metcalf & Metcalf. Family Clinic.

Metcalf, L. (2009) *The Field Guide to Counselling Toward Solutions: The Solution Focused School*. San Francisco: Jossey-Bass.

Ratner, H. (2003) Solution-Focused Therapy in Schools. In B. O'Connell and S. Palmer (Eds.) *Handbook of Solution-Focused Therapy*. London: Sage.

Ratner, H. (forthcoming) The Value of Scale Questions. In D. Yusuf (Ed.) *Solution Focused Practice with Children and Young People: A Celebration of Current Thinking and Applications*. London: Routledge.

Ratner, H., George, E. and Iveson, C. (2012) *Solution Focused Brief Therapy: 100 Key Points and Techniques*. London: Routledge.

Ratner, H. and Yusuf, D. (2015) *Brief Coaching with Children and Young People: A Solution Focused Approach*. London: Routledge.

Rhodes, J. and Ajmal, Y. (1995) *Solution Focused Thinking in Schools*. London: BT Press.
Shilts, L. (4th edition, 2013) The WOWW Program. In P. DeJong and I.K. Berg (Eds.) *Interviewing for Solutions*. Pacific Grove, CA: Brooks/Cole.
Young, S. (2009) *Solution-Focused Schools: Anti-Bullying and Beyond*. London: BT Press.

Part 2 How will we know we are at our best? Conversations with whole classes

13. Introduction: involving students

A class that is buzzing with activity and ideas is a great place to be for both staff and students. Inviting classes into constructive conversations about building the classroom environment that brings out the best in them can capture this energy and lay the foundations for doing more of what is working. The SF approach has a number of ideas that could be of use for teachers and their students in strengthening the co-operative elements of the class and guiding them towards success. These ideas can be used in short 5 minute conversations or the occasional longer discussion.

How classes describe themselves can bring motivation and optimism into what they do. When students have a vested interest in shaping how things are going, making their views visible can also encourage ownership. Even if not *all* the students are doing *all* of the things described *all* of the time, the fact that they are momentarily a part of a picture of success can offer them a different view of themselves and their possibilities.

14. Inviting students to step into their 'best version'

When we invite students to describe what the best version of their class will look like, 'How will we know that this class is at its best today/tomorrow/next week?' or 'What will we be noticing in this lesson that will tell us that we are working well together today?', we are also communicating a belief that this is attainable. As secondary students move through school and preparation for exams becomes more intense, the questions can be modified to accommodate this: 'If you could design a classroom environment that brings out the best in your learning in preparation for your exams, what would be happening?' A playful version is to ask students to design a classroom that would be guaranteed to make it impossible to learn. This is usually fun and full of colourful details which can then provide a basis for considering what the opposite would look like.

One answer is never enough; we need lots of examples

We want to build a rich picture. The clearer and more relevant the picture is, the easier it is to start seeing and noticing those behaviours and actions that already reside in the class but may not have been noticed. A good starting point could be '10 things that are already going well in this class' or '10 things that I might already be noticing'. This could then be followed by 'What else do you think you or I might be noticing during this next lesson? What else?'

Here is a list that a Year 6 class came up with:

- We are good at asking questions. At which point another child added: 'We want to find things out'.
- We listen to the teacher. *Cue additional question*: 'How will I know that you are listening?'
- If someone gets something wrong someone will help them.
- We sometimes tidy up things without being asked.
- If we are really interested in our work we can concentrate.
- If someone is being silly we tell the teacher.
- If someone is upset we try and help them.
- We don't always do this but we can be a good team like in our sports where we have to play together.
- We have good ideas.
- We remind each other that we have to do our Standard Assessment Tests (SATs), so we have to focus on our work and not distract each other.

A child then said that sometimes they weren't very good at focusing which prompted a discussion about the times when they were able to do it and what was different then. The class could have been asked: 'Imagine during the next lesson you suddenly became really good at focusing on your work and not being distracted, what will you and I be noticing?'

The inclusion of several details moves a discussion beyond students simply reiterating things they have been told or think we want to hear, towards the more unique thinking of individuals. We can then step back, carry on with the lesson and see what emerges. Creative ideas can lead to actions. The 'actions' might, in reality, look a little different from the original ideas, but it is the essence of 'being at our best' that we want students to take away from the initial discussion with maybe a few pointers in their heads as starters. The most productive way to follow up at the end of the lesson or the day would be an open question: 'What have we been pleased to notice?', rather than the more prescriptive: 'Let's go through the list'. This allows space for new successful behaviours to emerge, a bit like a phone upgrade where the original features are supplemented by additional attributes.

A supply teacher once described how he would start work with a new class by asking the students: 'How will we know that we are having a good day together? What will I notice you doing and what will you notice me doing?' The very fact that the teacher involved himself in the question provided a legitimacy for him to add his own ideas alongside those of the students. He wrote the ideas on the board at the front. During the first 15 minutes of the lesson, the teacher made sure he fed back to the students examples from their suggestions that he had observed. This both validated their contributions and was a further reminder of behaviours and expectations.

At the end of the day the teacher recapped by asking the students: 'What are the good things that happened today? What have you been most pleased to have noticed?' '*Most*' implies this is the tip of the iceberg and there were more things that could be talked about. Teachers can add what they themselves have noticed or ask the students to *guess* what they would have liked or been pleasantly surprised about. In this way the teacher was able to build a new description with the class of their successful behaviours that went beyond their initial ideas. It also avoided highlighting what had not worked. It gave a positive point of reference for the teacher to be able to discuss behaviour and a more energising approach to the challenge of working with a class he was not familiar with.

15. Being specific makes actions more accessible and possible

The more concrete and observable ideas are, the more students will be able to see and experience them. There are a number of ways to delineate the finer points of actions.

Stating what is wanted rather than what would be absent

A common answer to the question 'How will you know that you are at your best today?' is a variation of 'I won't be distracted'. We can't work towards nothing and if we rubbed out 'being distracted' there is a void that needs filling. Enquiring 'What will be happening instead?', 'What will be taking its place?' or 'What will you be doing instead?' encourages students to fill the vacant space with, for example, 'I will be more focused'. However, as will be shown, this still needs more work to make it specific and doable.

Breaking large ideas down into smaller parts

'Being more focused' will mean different things to different students. So, attaching our zoom lens, we would be curious about what being more focused *looks like* or how this *would show* today or in this lesson. In a similar way, when younger children talk about 'doing our work', we would be interested in what the observable signs of this would be by asking them to 'Show me what you will be doing when you are doing your work'. Each example of an action, such as putting their hands up, putting their head down and looking at their book or writing something, can be commented on: 'So you will have your book in front of you and be writing something'. In effect, we are helping the students break down the act of 'doing our work' into a series of small actions and behaviours.

Use the different activities to give prompts

There are also many sides to 'being more focused' which can be accessed through prompts about key times and activities in the school day. Students can be asked how this focus would show when they are getting their materials ready, when they are settling down, when they are working, when something is difficult or when someone is trying to distract them. Identifying time, place and context places the descriptions within the lived-in experience of the day-to-day classroom.

Be selective

It is not usually possible to pay attention to everything so the teacher can be selective about what they want students to notice or concentrate on more specifically, with a question such as: 'What will tell us that we are "communicating well" in this project work?' These could either be shared or kept private.

Conversely, students can be encouraged to be discerning about which of the things they have described they would like to turn the spotlight on. Looking at their ideas, in pairs, in small groups or as the whole class, they can be asked to consider:

- Which of these suggestions would be the most helpful to you in your learning?
- Which of these things do you think has the greatest impact on how well things go in the classroom?
- Which of these things would you like to do more of?

Students could also be invited to think about their own special way of contributing to things going well in the class and to consider what they will notice and what others will see if they were to do this.

Look at the benefits

Helping students to detail the benefits can help strengthen the importance of an action or behaviour. The more the benefits are understood, the more pertinent the discussion will be to their life in the classroom. Thus, in response to an idea, students can be invited to consider:

- How would that be good for you, your group, this class?
- What difference would that make to you, the students on your table, the class?

If the indication is that the effects would be minimal or absent, then it opens the way for a further question about what *would* be useful or what *would* make a difference.

16. The perspective of others

There are often other people in the school who are interested in how things are going for a class and it can be useful to help students think about what *they* will notice.

- What would the head teacher, head of year, your mother notice if they came into the classroom, that would tell them that this group or class is working well today?
- What will the students on your table or your friends notice about you that would tell them you are at your best this lesson?
- What will you be most pleased for others to notice?

Asking students to describe what they are doing through the eyes of others can also help them to translate something they might *think* they are doing, for example, 'making an effort', into more explicitly observable behaviours in the public social world. One of the great strengths of working with whole classes is the wealth of examples that reside there. If a student is struggling to understand or describe what 'making an effort' would look like, they can be set the task of observing the class for 5 minutes and seeing what other students do when they are making an effort.

Interactions

It is also true that actions rarely happen in isolation and students and staff are well versed in the 'he said this – so I said that – then he did this – so I did that' sequence. Given the social nature of learning in the classroom, it is sometimes useful to pay attention to the relationship aspects of class life. A useful sequence of questions might include:

- How will your teacher know that you are (for example) working well in your group?
- How will your teacher let you know that she has noticed (insert detail)?
- And if your teacher did show that she has noticed, what effect will this have on you?

Although this level of detail is not needed in every instance, there are occasions when it is sometimes worth excavating the smaller actions and interactions behind an original statement. Here is an extract from a discussion with a Year 6 class in preparation for their SATs later in the year showing some of the answers that members of the class offered.

Practitioner:	What will your teacher be noticing that will tell him that you are at your best in your learning over these next few weeks in getting ready for your SATs?
Student:	We would be working hard.
Practitioner:	Hmm. Ok. Can you give me an example of what your teacher will see that will tell him that you are working hard?
Another student:	He will see us doing lots of things.
Practitioner:	Can you pick one thing?
Student:	We will be more focused.
Practitioner:	You will be more focused. That's an interesting idea. How will this show? How will your teacher know that you are being more focused, even if you don't tell him? What will he see?
Student:	We will be looking at our work.
Practitioner:	Ok. What else will tell him that you are being more focused?
Student:	We will be answering questions.
Practitioner:	And would your teacher be pleased to notice these things? Looking at your work and answering questions?
Student:	Yes.
Practitioner:	How will you know that your teacher is pleased? What might he do that would let you know that he is pleased?
Student:	He might say something nice.

Practitioner:	And would you like that?
Student:	Yes.
Practitioner:	What difference will it make to you? When your teacher says something nice, what might you then do?
Student 1:	It will make us want to do more.
Student 2:	It will make us feel clever.
Practitioner:	Ok. And how will your teacher know that you are feeling clever?

17. How do you keep the students thinking and looking?

Expanding on what works

In addition to recognising and praising achievements, there is more to be learnt about *how* they were achieved. Many of the ideas described in the 'at your best version' may already be happening. Classes can be asked to list, describe or discuss the things that they are already doing all together, in groups or in pairs. This could be followed by a further skills- and resource-based discussion:

- *Process*: How come you decided to do things in that way?
- *Strategies and competence*: How did you get that to work?
- *Benefits*: What are your good reasons for doing things in this way?
- *Resilience*: How come you managed to keep going?
- *Identity*: What did you learn about yourself by managing to do that?

Increasing the awareness of students as to what they do well makes their skills more available to them and leads to more positive outcomes.

Continually adding to and refining

When students start to think and describe themselves 'at their best' they are more predisposed to continue to notice things that fit with this version of themselves. The more they notice the more they will begin to define themselves in this way.

In a Year 7 class, groups were asked to describe what being at their best *today* would look like, what they would notice about themselves and others. Their ideas were displayed on the tables and when a student came up with another observation, they would check to see if it was already written down before adding it. In this way, the students' lists became a dynamic record of all that was good in what they were doing. If the students had experienced some challenges it would still be possible to ask:

- How did you manage that in a way that was still good for you and the learning of the group?
- What ways did you find of dealing with any difficulty which might be useful in the future?
- Suppose things started to get back on track again, what will you, others and I notice?

18. Using scales

Building scale discussions around 'the best version'

An initial discussion can also be followed up with periodic scaling reviews which can bring together all the main elements of a SF conversation: the aspirations of 'at your best', helping students to celebrate their current achievements and locating where to go to next. Scales can be drawn, represented by objects or walked along as they collect the views of a whole class around a specified area.

Taking 10 as standing for 'the best class we can hope to be' or the best version of whatever has been discussed, students can be asked to indicate the number that represents where they would put the class or themselves today by raising their hands, physically standing at a number or even writing privately on a piece of paper. Their numbers can be used to generate an average or left as a range. The class can then reflect on what they have noticed that has been working: 'So on average the class thinks things are at a 6. Let's come up with a list of things that you have noticed to put things there and not lower'. As their list grows, the class can be asked to consider those things that have made the most difference, pleased them the most, that they think their teacher would be most surprised about, and so on. At the same time, students do not always have to be asked to qualify a number, as simply giving one can encourage reflection.

Students can also be asked: 'Let's imagine that tomorrow, next week, next term we move one point higher. How will we know? What will we be doing? What will we be seeing?' and developing as much detail in the descriptions as possible. Inviting students into what they *might* be doing is different from asking them to specifically detail what they *will or should* be doing. Take, for example, a Year 8 tutor who realised that she had used a scale in completely the wrong way when addressing a class whose behaviour had been unacceptable. She candidly reported that her question, 'Why aren't you at an 8 in your behaviour? What should you be doing?' turned the scale into a tool for telling off and in doing so, removed the curiosity and discussion which allows change to be driven by the students themselves. She felt that there were more obvious signs of improvement when she kept the activity of 'telling off' separate from the activity of building intrinsic motivation through descriptions.

If students working in groups are asked to give a group number, there is always the possibility that competition can creep in when these numbers become a symbol of 'winning' or 'being better than others' rather than a route to describing behaviours. Nothing ever works all the time, so this would usually be taken as a sign to do something different. For example, asking each group for *details* about what is working well, and then asking for a number about the class as a whole. Or just sticking to lists and descriptions.

Occasional scaling reviews

What marks scales out as such a wonderful support to ongoing dialogues is the multitude of different ways and different questions that can be used to help students reflect and grow. A head teacher who had used a 'this is the best class in the borough' scale with a Year 4 class, would occasionally pop his head around the classroom door and ask where things were on the scale today, this morning, this period. Sometimes he varied the question:

- Where were things today when they were at their highest? Tell me 5 things that were happening.
- Where would you like to see yourselves this afternoon? Tell me 4 things your teacher will see.

The head teacher felt it was about engagement: 'We can tell them, or we can listen to what they have to say and actively involve them in working out the best way forward.'

If the numbers are lower, classes can be asked for the small things that have still been ok, how they have stopped things from getting lower and signs of moving back up their scale again. The principle is to identify those things that will be useful for further progress.

19. How do we record these discussions?

The simplest answer to this is whatever fits with what you want to achieve. Talking with classes about their best version might lead to the emergence of actions not explicitly mentioned but implied or inspired by the conversation. The teacher can therefore observe what happens and prepare to be surprised!

In the Introduction we talked about a class of children building an ever expanding list of what good learning looked like in their classroom which was displayed at the front of the class. What often happens is that the first descriptions are broad and familiar. As a list grows, less obvious and more unique ideas will begin to emerge.

The orchestral conductor and teacher Benjamin Zander gives another example of the use of written material. He describes how he gave the following instruction to 30 graduate students at the first class in September at the New England Conservatory:

> Each student in this class will get an A for the course. However, there is one requirement that you must fulfil to earn this grade. Sometime during the next two weeks, you must write me a letter dated next May, which begins with the words, "Dear Mr Zander, I got my A because..." and in this letter you are to tell, in as much detail as you can, the story of what will have happened to you by next May that is in line with this extraordinary grade.
>
> (Zander and Zander 2000: 27)

He goes on to reproduce some of the letters he received, and then adds: 'Small wonder that I approach each class with the greatest eagerness, for this is a class consisting entirely of A students and what is more delightful than spending an afternoon among the stars?' (Zander and Zander op cit. 30).

20. 5 minute versions

When time is tight, small accessible structures that are built into the daily routine of classrooms can set in motion a progressive dialogue that can pick up new ideas and expand along the way.

Using short lists with whole classes

Short lists can be inserted anywhere during a lesson and are a useful tool for re-engaging a class if they have gone a bit off track. People sometimes worry about imposing a number. Asking for more than one detail demonstrates our belief in the class and students are often more likely to get there if they hear confidence on our part.

   Pointing towards successful futures:

- 3 things we will notice today, or the rest of this period, that will tell us this class is at its best.
- 5 signs that will tell you that the lesson is going well.
- What would be the first 4 signs that things have improved from yesterday?

Paying attention to successful pasts:

- Tell me 4 things that have gone well today.
- What 5 things have you been pleased to see your group doing this morning?
- What are 4 things you think I will have been pleased to notice so far this lesson?
- Name 3 things that have helped you keep yourself on track for achieving your targets.

Providing the opportunity for short reflections between students

It is the regularity of reflections that can make the most difference. A secondary humanities teacher compiled a list of questions for students to think about what was working for them. When there were a few minutes at the beginning or end of a period, the teacher would pick a question for students to consider individually or to facilitate short discussions between students. The students sometimes recorded their answers at the back of their books. Examples of the type of questions she would choose from include:

- Something in my learning this week that has surprised me in a good way is … .
- One thing I have been doing differently in my studying this week is … .
- Something I now feel confident about in my learning is … . What I have done that I think has helped this along is … .

Versions that could also be used at primary level might include:

- My top tips on learning (or my top tips on *my* learning).
- My best lesson. 5 things that made it so good. 4 things I did. 3 things the teacher did.

- One thing I did that helped my learning today is ... .
- Something I will be pleased to notice, or notice more of, tomorrow is ....

Younger children can be asked more simply for one good thing they did. Initially teachers can have a range of statements prepared such as: 'I wrote a lot today' or 'I kept quiet while I was working'. As the statements are read out, the children can put their hands up, go and stand on a circle, put a marble in a jar or stick the statement in their books to indicate the one that described what they had done. It would be hoped that over time the children would start to generate their own unique descriptions of behaviours.

21. Talking with a whole class when there has been a difficulty

A Year 5 teacher commented that she could see how the SF ideas could be used when things are going smoothly, but was unsure how they would apply if it was necessary to talk with a whole class when there had been an incident. Shortly afterwards, her class was sent back from their music lesson as the teacher had refused to carry on with the lesson due to their behaviour. In addition to the sanctions and systems that schools follow there is also a time and a place for helping a class get back on track. The following section outlines a joint session carried out with the class teacher immediately after the class had returned.

The teacher began by asking: 'What's been happening? Was the whole lesson difficult or were there some good things as well?' This offered an opening for the class to describe the situation from their point of view, rather than the teacher solely speaking about the concerns of the music teacher. It provided a pause in the flow of events and the teacher got to hear about a range of desirable things that had happened which could have been lost or ignored: the class had settled quickly and the first half of the lesson had been fine. These were good things that could be complimented and for those students who had behaved well this was especially important.

Setting up a scale and finding out about the 10: A visual scale using the two sides of the room was set up. The '10' side represented the best music lesson possible and the '0' side represented the worst. The class was asked to describe what the 10 would look like and they began to build a collective vision of what would 'be right' rather than having to explain 'what was wrong'. There was no need for blame or justification or for students to have to agree. Instead, they were invited to start designing a solution where each unique contribution could be included. The greater the number of possibilities made available, the greater the likelihood of success. Every so often, students were invited to consider the benefits of certain ideas. For example, asking: 'What difference would this make to you?' gave meaning to potential actions.

Looking at today and hearing more about the good things: The students were asked to raise their hands at the number which best represented their view of how things had been in the actual music lesson. Eight students indicated 0. The rest were spread between 1 and 4 with one student on 5 and another on 7. The students were then invited to share in more detail some of the small things that had been all right. Rather than isolating those students who had misbehaved, this helped to re-engage them back into the group as students generally have a good idea about what is acceptable, even if they have not directly done these things themselves. Those students who had put things at a 0 were still invited to contribute if they wished, which six of them did.

Signs of progress: The students were asked if they wanted the next music lesson to go better and were given three options: yes; 50/50; no ('I am fine if things stay the same'). Most students said yes, a few said 50/50 and a couple said no. This might sound like an odd question, but it enabled all of the class to engage in a description of a future when the class was not in trouble from their own viewpoint and level of enthusiasm. Honouring this full spectrum of views, the class were then invited to think about the small signs that would tell them that things were going better in music. The students who had indicated that they were ok with things were asked to think about those things that they would want to keep the same. Implicit within this question is the assumption that change is not usually about changing everything, just some things. Many of the ideas were about settling down quicker, helping each other more and smiling at the teacher 'as he might like that'.

No Action Plan: There was deliberately no action plan. The seeds of change had been sown. If left to choose, students will often come up with creative ideas of their own that go beyond the conversation. Thus, we gave the students the benefit of the doubt and trusted the process of the discussion.

An alternative idea would be to set up a 'secret society' whereby students are asked to sit and think to themselves about one thing they think they can do, should they so wish, to help the class move towards a 10 on the scale. However, they are instructed to keep it a secret and just see who notices! This removes all pressure to act and offers future opportunities to ask: 'What have you noticed other students doing in this class today that has been good?'

How the children responded

The entire conversation took just over 10 minutes. It was then playtime and as we all know this is a sacred time that cannot be delayed! However, as the class filed out seven students remained, all wanting to say something. One student was keen to make it clear that she did not want things to change because her behaviour had been ok. A second student observed that the class did not adjust well to new teachers: 'I think we have a problem with that'. Another student pointed a finger and said: 'I know what you are doing. You are positive when it's positive and positive when it is negative'. It is always important to check out such statements to see whether the student thinks this is a good thing and on balance she thought it was.

What the teacher thought

The teacher was surprised at how readily the students had engaged in the discussion given that they were 'in trouble'. The fact that some students had wanted to carry on during their playtime indicated to her that they were still thinking, processing and interested. She felt the discussion had directly supported school values identified in the school improvement plan, such as:

- *Pupils to manage their own behaviour*: The students had a clear idea about what was and was not acceptable behaviour and took responsibility for what was happening.
- *Positive learning behaviours*: The students had listened well to each other, respected their differing views and built on each other's ideas.

I think one of the main differences this has made to me is to slow down the process. I also realise that even when things are difficult it is not all bad. The questions have helped me to think about how to ask about things, trying to get more information, for example, 'What else?' And the children can apply this to lots of other things.

(class teacher)

We are often told that SF methods 'are all very well but who has the time?' The comment above about 'slowing down the process' would seem to confirm this criticism. However, as a hare once discovered, slower can be quicker. This classroom intervention that turned 'hot water into a bath' took only 10 minutes and quite possibly saved 10 times that amount in the long run.

Postscript

In the weeks that followed, the students from this class would still stop the practitioner in the corridor and refer to 'that scale thing' along with their current rating in music and usually a detail about something that had gone well. Five months later, the class performed a set of instrumental pieces and singing for the school. They were outstanding.

5 minute scale conversation with a class

A broad 0-10 scale where 10 is the best and 0 is the worst. State what the scale is related to and build a short description of what the 10 will look like.
Where would you put things at the moment? List 15 good things that are happening.
How will you know that things are 1 point higher? 10 signs.
Optional questions
What number would you like to be saying? What would be happening at this point?
What number would you give your best lesson as a class over the past two weeks and what good things were happening at this time?

22. Variations of scales in the classroom

Just as there are a multitude of questions, so there are a multitude of ways that scales can be utilised. They can be visual, using numbers, pictures or objects, physical scales which students can walk along or playful scales using interests such as football teams or music artists. Each point on the scale can be a symbolic representation of a number of behaviours or actions so that 'I am Beyonce today' becomes a euphemism for how things are going.

Snapshot scales

Keeping students thinking and talking about themselves as learners can, at the same time, provide feedback to staff about what methods and approaches seem to work best. 'Snapshot scales' offer an excellent at-a-glance overview of where students are at in their work. 10 can stand for 'I have fully completed my work', or describe a student's confidence or understanding of a topic or learning objective. In addition to the stated criteria for success, asking students how they and the teacher will know they have fully understood, helps to further clarify expectations and outcomes. Finding out what has helped so far in building a student's confidence or understanding in the topic can also highlight methods and approaches that have worked well.

In a similar way, a Year 11 tutor set up a scale with her tutor group to monitor how on top of their work they felt. She was conscious of the pressures of GCSE exams and wanted to find a way to keep an eye on how her students were managing. 10 represented 'fine, on track' and 0 'going under'. At each morning registration when their names were called out, the students were asked to give a number alongside affirming they were present. A low number repeated over a couple of days would alert the teacher to check in with the student. An unexpected by-product was the care shown by friends when they heard one of their friends was struggling. What the students reported was that it was a lot easier to convey in a number, rather than words, that they were experiencing difficulties.

Cross referencing scales across a number of situations

Scales can be used across a number of different situations and the disparity in numbers can be used to look at what is different at those times when things are going better. A Year 9 form tutor wanted to look with her tutor group at their behaviour across the school day. A scaling record was set up for each subject teacher to numerically describe the class's behaviour at the end of every lesson with, if there was time, a couple of things they had liked. The tutor used the numbers to build a discussion with her form about the difference in their behaviour across the lessons and in particular what contributed to the higher numbers. If we are to encourage students to take ownership of their behaviour, then it is important to help them understand how they can affect outcomes.

Scales in an assembly

A secondary head teacher (Richard Paul, personal communication) outlined his use of a scale with a complete cohort of Year 8 students. He was interested in their views on behaviour in the school and was using them as a panel of experts. He set up a scale where 10 was described as utopia and 0 as carnage. The entire hall was asked to indicate where they would put things currently. A couple of students were then asked to talk about their numbers which were both around the 5 or 6 level. One comment was that students were already being responsive when requested by staff to alter their behaviour in the corridor. A sign of progress would be for these requests not to need to be made. The head teacher was delighted by both the numbers and these observations. It suggested that the students themselves had higher aspirations for their behaviour. In true SF fashion the head teacher ended the conversation with an affirmation that the students would know how to sort it out.

23. Creating opportunities for appreciation in the classroom

Some classrooms can be difficult places for students to voice opinions or ideas in the co-creation of how they would like things to be. When there is a culture of negativity among the students, it can quickly suppress the quieter and less confident members of a class and chip away at the self-esteem and creativity of all the students. In these situations it might be necessary to create opportunities for students to practice the art of noticing and naming the good things that are happening and experience the consequent pleasure of hearing what is valued.

Observations

With older students especially, the tone can often be best set in the first instance through observations. The following ideas draw on the WOWW principle of Working on What Works (Berg and Shilts 2005; Ratner et al. 2012; Shilts 2013), seeking out what is working and feeding this back. This can reveal to classes qualities they can begin to recognise in themselves. The observations can be of a short duration and carried out by the teacher or an additional member of staff.

Classes can be asked to guess how many good things they think an observer will find or they can just be told that the observer is looking for all the good things happening in the class. One Year 8 class in a secondary school guessed that only between 0–8 things would be observed in 20 minutes. Thirty-two things were found and there is something about the volume of things noticed that carries an important message to the students. Feedback was both class-based, thus increasing group identity: 'This is a class that is thoughtful and has the capacity to surprise your teacher with your answers'; and individually-based, thus increasing individual confidence and competence: 'I noticed students on this table were good at predicting what the teacher wanted and started before she needed to ask'. An accumulation of little things can often be more effective and useful than a couple of big and splendid things. One teacher commented after an observation of her class:

> We are so often looking at what is wrong that we often ignore what is going well. And you found so many small things such as noticing the students who were thinking before they wrote things or how quietly they used their equipment. These can be just as useful as big things.
>
> (class teacher)

Highlighting competence and effectiveness is empowering for teachers and students and also provides fertile information on which to build change. Imagine going to a meeting with some ideas about what already works with these students or the conditions that bring out the best in this class; time can then be profitably spent looking at how to do more of this or make it even more effective. If additional support is being sought, it can also provide evidence or ideas about *how* this support could be deployed.

Students as observers

Placing students in a position of observing a class provides them with a completely different view of what is happening and the chance to step into a different role in reporting back. It might also provide the opportunity for the teacher to learn more about the class through the eyes of its students.

A teacher of a Year 10 class was interested in the idea of student observation. Tina was a popular and influential member of the class who spent a lot of her time in the internal exclusion room due to her disruptive behaviour. The teacher decided to ask Tina if she could help him by observing what was working well in the class: what she noticed the students doing and what difference this made. He was taken aback by just how accurate Tina's observations were and how much pleasure was shown by the class when listening to the feedback. The fact that Tina requested to do more observations was an added bonus given how settled and involved she had been with the lesson. Placing students like Tina in positions of expertise can have a significant impact in helping them to re-define themselves as someone who has useful and interesting things to contribute.

In a primary school Year 5 and 6 children are occasionally co-opted to provide observations in other classes or to observe alongside younger children, acting as their scribe and pointing things out to them. Teachers can also appoint 'secret observers' to note down and then feedback the good things they are noticing and hearing during a lesson. This is a fun way to keep students noticing and naming.

'Sparkling moments' and the compliment game

At a primary level, a catchy phrase such as 'sparkling moments' (White 1998: 202) can provide a short-hand route into sharing what is working well. Sparkles can be general, for example, ending the day with '3 things that sparkled' or related to a specific activity or theme such as 'a sparkly moment at break time' or 'how we worked well together'. In one class students would often comment: 'I am going to give my sparkle today to (insert student's name) because (insert an observation)'.

> 'Sparkling moments' changed the dialogue in the classroom from one of criticism to one where students enjoyed hearing about what others had to say.
>
> (class teacher)

> I always looked forward to hearing my name as I knew someone was going to say something nice.
>
> (Year 6 student)

The 'compliment game' is a more formal activity which provides a context for students to hear themselves described in ways that they have perhaps not heard before. A statement reflecting a quality or value that is important in the classroom can be read out: 'I am thinking of someone who is good at finding ways out of a difficulty'. The class is asked to guess who the teacher is thinking of and give their evidence. For example, 'I am thinking of Katya because she always has good ideas'. If it *is* Katya, then she can be congratulated. If it is not Katya, she can still be congratulated for being chosen by the student and for the observation made. Sometimes the teacher will agree it was a good guess and outline something else he or she knows about Katya, but state that on this occasion he or she is thinking of someone else. The teacher can keep going for a few rounds or until the students have guessed correctly. In one Year 4 class, the teacher eventually revealed it was Mitchell she was thinking of as someone who was very helpful. He looked at the teacher and said with a huge smile: 'I didn't see *that* coming!'

A variation of this is to have a board with a weekly 'I am thinking of someone who ...' statement. Students can make nominations plus their reasons using post-it notes. At the end of the week the teacher can read these out and let the class know who she was thinking about.

> We like what we are seeing, it is a way of looking for things to celebrate. Students are talking to each other in a different way. The class are showing care towards each other. I love the way the children are lifting each other up.
>
> (Year 3 teacher)

References

Berg, I.K. and Shilts, L. (2005) Keeping the Solutions inside the Classroom. *ASCA School Counsellor*, July/August.

Ratner, H., George, E. and Iveson, C. (2012) *Solution Focused Brief Therapy: 100 Key Points and Techniques*. London: Routledge.

Shilts, L. (2013) The WOWW Program. In P. DeJong and I.K. Berg (Eds.) *Interviewing for Solutions* (4th edn). Pacific Grove, CA: Brooks/Cole.

White, M. (1998) *Re-Authoring Lives: Interviews & Essays*. South Australia: Dulwich Centre Publications.

Zander, R.S. and Zander, B. (2000) *The Art of Possibility*. New York: Penguin.

Part 3   Individual work

24. Introduction: principles

This chapter explores many different ways to build uniquely shaped conversations to support any student in discovering how to bring out the best in themselves, whether their behaviour or their learning is the focus. When we use SF language and thinking in our interactions with students, we are looking to invite a different way of viewing things that will open up options and build a shared way forward. This sometimes takes a little work! Take, for example, Tony, a Year 11 student who had just attended a session on study skills.

Practitioner:	How did it go?
Tony:	It was really good.
Practitioner:	What did you like about it?
Tony:	The guy who did it was really funny and he made us laugh.
Practitioner:	And what was the most useful thing you took away from it?
Tony:	What do you mean? (*looking puzzled*)
Practitioner:	Well, it was about study skills and I was curious about what you heard that might have been useful to you.
Tony:	I don't know. (*looking blankly*)
Practitioner:	What sorts of things was the presenter talking about?
Tony:	I don't know. (*shrug*)

This is not to say the presenter did not have a lot of good ideas or that Tony was necessarily being obtuse. Rather that something else was needed to bridge the gap between what was presented and Tony's own world and experience. The following ideas are not intended to replace the procedures or systems that schools follow, but to augment dialogues to create energy and movement in even the toughest of conversations.

Key things to bear in mind

- If a student is in the room then they want something, even if, in the first instance, it is expressed as a negative, the wish to be rid of something rather than achieve something.
- Finding a point of motivation for the student is a crucial opening into a conversation; it is where the most potential for change resides.

- Establishing a focus on what is wanted (instead of investigating what is going wrong) represents an important step in elucidating behaviours that will support a forward motion towards this.
- If we are to encourage sustainable changes, then there has to be personal input from the student. When a student says 'yes' to everything, it often means adults are doing the hard thinking while the student is working out the quickest way to exit the conversation and the room.
- A belief that the student has what it takes (until proven otherwise) to make the changes they want enables us to remain optimistic in even the most difficult of circumstances and to go the extra mile in helping them discover their skills and strengths.

It is far from easy to stick to these five principles, especially when faced with an extremely challenging student, but by doing so we guard against the danger of our own sense of hopelessness and the consequent risk of giving up on the student.

25. Getting started: building a common direction

It is usually the case that most individual conversations with students will have been instigated by the school. It is less usual for a student to present themselves to a member of staff and say: 'I need to sort myself out'. Consider Tyrone, a Year 8 student, who was causing disruption in most of his lessons and was economical with words when asked to consider this. The practitioner was asked to meet him at his Spanish lesson as he was unlikely to remember that a discussion had been scheduled. Tyrone's apparent delight in being released from his lesson turned into a wall of silence as they walked down the corridor. From his shoulder gymnastics, the practitioner ascertained that he had no idea who had suggested they should speak or what his teachers were wanting. It was hard, with so little feedback, to determine even the tiniest glimpse of anything that Tyrone had an interest in discussing. Given such a situation, what are the possibilities for inviting a student into a conversation that feels less like paddling upstream in a dinghy with a slow puncture? We will return to Tyrone later in the chapter.

The first step is to establish a common direction: finding something that both school and students ultimately would work towards. The second step is to explore what this will look like.

Closed to open questions

A simple approach is to use a closed question which can then lead to a more open question. The closed part defines the context for the discussion, the open part invites the student to step into the conversation.

- It seems like things have not been going well in your learning or studying lately. Would you like things to go better? 'Yes'.
- It seems school has been pretty miserable for you lately. Would you like to be happier at school? 'Yes'.
- You want to be off report? 'Yes.' So if our talking today somehow helped you to get off report, that would be useful? 'Yes'.

A 'yes' response in answer to the closed question is not simply an acceptance on the part of the student about what they should or should not be doing. The purpose is to provide a doorway into a potential conversation. Once momentum has been established, it is easier to build a dialogue.

A head teacher, feeling overwhelmed with the number of urgent post-it notes on his desk, was not best pleased about having to deal with two 9-year-old girls for whom a dispute that had begun in the playground had then continued into the classroom. As he had so little time, he began by asking the girls if they would *like* things to be sorted out. One agreed, one didn't. So he sat them apart outside his room whilst he dealt with the most pressing issues. Ten minutes later, at the third time of enquiring, he received an agreement from both of the girls that they would like things to be resolved. Instead of looking at what needs to change, the outcome orientation of SFP will be on what things will be like when they *are* changed. Thus, the next 5 minutes were spent finding out what would be different when things *were* sorted out. A picture emerged of two friends playing together and helping each other in class. The head teacher also asked what the teacher and other students would notice that would tell them that things were better. The girls went back to class with a promise to return at lunchtime and each tell him three good things that had been happening, leaving a head teacher with time and energy to spare.

Twin tracking

Staff sometimes ask about what happens when a student has to make a change that is dictated by someone else. Bearing in mind the importance of finding a point of motivation for the student, the following ideas around 'twin tracking' (Ratner et al. 2012: 90) can sometimes offer an opening. If we think in terms of the student's track as being the 'first track' (what they want), the task then becomes to find ways in which the 'second track' (what others want) can be interwoven to open up opportunities.

Once a clear statement has been made to the student about what others want, the student could be asked to consider what difference such a change would make to *them*. 'Suppose for a moment that you did start attending your lessons, what difference would it make to you?' A common initial reply might be the absence of something: 'The school would not be on my back' or 'I would not be on report'. Generally speaking, even with responses such as these, once it has been established what is in it for the student to achieve certain outcomes, then the talk can swing back towards the 'first track', that is, framed in terms of what *they* want.

> Teacher: And that is something you would like, for the school to get off your back?
> Student: Yes.
> Teacher: What difference would it make to you if they were off your back?
> Student: I would be getting on with my life without them being in my face.

After exploring what 'getting on' would look like, the teacher can ask: 'What would be the first signs that would tell you that you are on track for getting the school off your back?' and add questions about what the school would notice: 'What would your teachers be noticing about you that would tell them they could back off from you?', 'How would you know they had noticed?'

Viewing what will be good for them in their terms can offer the student a different way of considering what is being required. Another tack is to use a both/and perspective: 'What would be the signs that things were going better in a way that was right for you *and* for the school?'

A student might be taking a 'couldn't care less' attitude to their learning. 'I hate maths and I won't do any work'. It might help for the teacher to have a conversation with the student and others in the group about the possible value knowing maths, or getting good grades, could make to their lives and their future. The intention would not, of course, be to make the student love maths, so a twin tracking question could be: 'Let's say you are making some progress in maths in a way that is right for you and the school, what would be the smallest signs of that?'

In more challenging situations, the student could be asked for their views on the *consequences* of things not changing in the way that is being required. If this is something that they wish to avoid, then again the conversation can return to the first track which, in this case, could include questions such as:

'What are the minimum changes the school would need to see in order for (insert consequence) not to occur?'

'How confident are you that you can avoid (insert consequence)? What do you know about yourself that gives you this much confidence?'

If the student is adamant that they will continue as things are even knowing the consequences, then attention can be paid to how they will know that they are dealing and managing this in the way that is the best for them.

26. Building virtual pathways to success

Building on the 'yes' response

In the above example with the 9-year-old girls, the head teacher explored what 'things being sorted' would look like. For the student where things have not been going well in their learning, we could ask: 'Suppose tomorrow things were to go better, what will you and others notice?' For the student who wants to be happier in school we could ask: 'How would your teacher know that you are happier?'

Any variation of a 'better day, a good day, a day when you are at your best' is an invitation into the preferred future. It is an optimistic framework that will fit most students and likely be more motivating than 'sorting out your behaviour' or 'settling to your learning', yet any discussion about 'better days' will encompass many useful behaviours. By asking about a day going well, we are communicating an expectation that it can happen and a belief that it is within the student's capabilities.

Increasing the observability of details

Increasing the observability of details optimises the likelihood that students will, so to speak, gain access to them. Most readers will be familiar with the notion of SMART goals (Specific, Measurable, Attainable, Realistic and Timely) to aid thinking. Here is a SF adaptation:

- Small: What will be the tiniest signs of this?
- Measurable: How will you know? How will others know?
- Action-orientated: What will you be doing? How will that show? What will others notice?
- Range of possible outcomes and routes: What else will you notice that will be signs of you at your best? What else will tell others that things are moving forward?
- Timely: What will you be noticing different by the end of this week?

A good rule of thumb is to think: 'Can I picture this happening?' Vague descriptions are hard to see, hard to measure and hard to evaluate.

Exploring the interactions

Interactional questions are also key to building a supportive environment around individual behaviours that we would like to see more of. A teacher in a Pupil Referral Unit was helping John to attach a forward focus to what a better afternoon would look like following a difficult morning. When John answered: 'I will be doing my work', the teacher first asked: 'How will I know that you are doing your work?', followed by: 'How will you know that I have *noticed* that you are doing your work?'

Making sure we are building descriptions related to a solution and not the problem

When students state something that *won't* be happening, for example, 'I won't be getting into fights', this is still a problem-related outcome. 'What will be happening *instead* of getting into fights?' or 'What *difference* will this make?' are intended to uncover a tangible indicator that is related to a solution rather than a problem. An example might be: 'I will be getting on better with friends'. To simply locate the future as 'avoiding fights' means that the better things are only thought of in the context of fighting. It ties the description to the problem. Building a description around a 'day getting on better with friends' will include a much wider description of a day where it is less likely that fighting will occur.

The use of narrative

Focusing in detail on the first 5 minutes of a lesson or the day, or sequentially tracking through a day, can set the scene and tone from which other desirable things can follow. Locating the description firmly and realistically in the world of the student moves it from being a fantasy towards a narrative where the student can picture themselves doing and saying actual things that could happen.

A Year 4 teacher was worried about taking Jacob on a trip given past experiences of outings and his generally unsettled behaviour in the classroom. A couple of days before the trip, she posed a question to him: 'It is our trip on Friday. I would like us to have a good day together. Is that something that you would like too?' Jacob agreed. If Jacob had said *no*, which is unlikely, then it could have led to a second question about what the student *would* like to happen on Friday. The teacher then asked: 'Suppose Friday turns out to be a good day for both of us. What will it look like and be like?' Although Jacob did not find it easy at first to picture his Friday, the teacher provided gentle prompts such as: 'What will be happening as we are waiting for the coach, travelling on the coach, getting off the coach?' and lots of 'What else?' questions. As Jacob's ideas began to flow, he asked the teacher if she could write them on a piece of paper. Her favourite response was to the question: 'How would you know that I had noticed these things?' to which Jacob commented: 'You wouldn't be rubbing your head so much!' Jacob also mentioned that other children would smile or want to sit next to him. On the morning of the trip, Jacob asked if he could have his 'list' which he sat and read through and proudly showed to some of the other children, before returning it to his teacher.

There is always a concern that a list can translate into a series of 'must do' behaviours that the student has to perform in order for a good day to happen, rather than provide a platform from which a good day can emerge. There are several things that can help:

- Firstly, if the student has come up with almost all of the contributions then this represents their ideas.
- Secondly, how we end the conversation. If the student leaves with the notion that the day being spoken about can be a good day, it may help to promote actions which make this more likely to be a reality. Thus, 'Good luck. I look forward to a day of surprises' leaves an opening for a wide range of behaviours to emerge, rather than 'Let's see how many of the things on the list you do on Friday'.
- Thirdly, how we follow up the discussion. If we say at the end of the day in question: 'So what were the good things that happened today?' the broadness of the question encourages the student to pick out and describe anything that they have noticed. A new 'list' could then be drawn up, this time representing a record of all the things the student *can* do.

At the end of the trip, the day had gone better than the class teacher could have hoped. She was smiling as she said: 'I am perhaps a little shocked. For one day, I saw my preferred future and Jacob lived his best hopes for the trip. I see this little glimmer as a starting point. I know there is more to come'.

Many roads lead to Rome

As a description unfolds, we will look to make available many different routes to change and difference and to build descriptions of a life that could support these changes.

Take, for example, a teacher who wants to have a discussion with a student who has been very distracted in their lesson. The teacher could start with a statement about the problem along the lines of 'That seemed to be a difficult lesson!' followed by a question: 'Would you like the next lesson to go better?' Unless the student states that they would like another difficult lesson, there are then several possibilities (and note that these can be pursued separately or together):

- Possibility 1: 'Suppose the next lesson does go better, what would this look like?' If only a couple of minutes are available, this might be the most expedient area of enquiry.
- Possibility 2: 'How would you know on your way to school tomorrow that this was going to be a day when you will be having better lessons?' This invites the student into describing a pattern of behaviours and thoughts within which better lessons are more likely to occur.
- Possibility 3: 'Suppose tomorrow is a good day with lessons going better, what difference will this make to you?' This embeds 'better lessons' into the wider context of the student's life and thus highlights possibilities beyond having a good lesson.
- Possibility 4: 'If tomorrow turned out to be a really good day how would your mum know when you got home?' This widens the discussion to include important relationships in the student's life and the ripple effect of behaviour.

Ideas for younger students

Younger students can be asked to build a description using words or pictures. A dynamic version which can bring a sense of fun and surprise into the students' worlds is to set a context whereby they can discover their best version through 'doing'. For example:

- Acting as if – role playing themselves at their best and observing what they do.
- Acting like – students can be asked to think of someone they admire such as a sports person, historical figure or whoever they decide, and describe their qualities. 'So, if Mo Farah were doing (insert task) what would you notice?' They can then be asked to imagine they are this person as they go about their work and see what happens.
- Younger children can be asked to imagine they have a superpower that helps them with their learning and explore, through doing, what this will look like.

5 minute conversation prompts

Suppose you are at your best (insert period of time or area being discussed).
What will you see? 4 details
What will others see? 3 details
What will be the smallest things you will be doing? 2 details
What difference will doing these things make? 1 thing
For any of the details you can further enquire:
What would that look like? How would that show? What difference would that make?

27. Resource-based discussions

Change is encouraged when we help a person draw on their resources. Arguably 'change' is the wrong word as that implies the *person* changes, while we see it as the person simply doing more of what they can do already. As people discover their own resources so they can make changes to what they do themselves. This is a fundamental aspect of SFP and will show up in every conversation.

Starter questions could include:

- Think about a time when you have been at your best this week, this term.
- Think about a time when you felt a sense of pride or achievement this week.
- What was your best bit of work recently?

We would then find out as much as we can about what was happening at these times. Validating and highlighting small things, that if repeated could make a big difference, ensures that useful ideas are not missed or dismissed as something that 'I just do'.

- How did you learn that? How did you do that? *(Reveals strategies)*
- How did you know what to do first and what to do next? *(Identifies a reasoned approach)*
- What were the 3 most important things you did? *(Encourages evaluative reflections)*
- What were the smallest things you noticed yourself doing that were helpful? *(Elevates small yet useful details)*
- What was your method of making (insert detail) work? *(Emphasises personal agency)*
- What was your way of overcoming any difficulties? *(Reinforces their resilient qualities)*

As we are helping students to tell a different story about themselves in the here and now, so we can also help them to build on this story in the future. However, students do not automatically make the link.

Jamil, a Year 9 student was experiencing huge difficulties in completing assignments due to what the school described as 'a total lack of organisation'. Jamil himself freely owned this description, adding that he did not like doing the work and mostly could not be bothered. The SF practitioner asked him what he *did* like doing and he began talking about his passion and support for the Arsenal football team. It turned out that he had devised an elaborate home and away tracker system for matches which involved cross referencing with other teams and an encyclopaedic knowledge of everything that was relevant to his team. The conversation then sought to break down into small steps what he did, his useful methods for recording things and the strategies he used to help him remember things. Finally, the practitioner looked at what Jamil would notice if these skills somehow worked themselves into his school life. The 'Arsenal approach' to his assignments made such sense that he could seriously have been running his own tuition sessions for other students.

2 minute conversation prompts

> Even a brief discussion in passing with a student about something they have done well or been pleased about so far that day can focus attention on what is potentially useful.
> What was your best lesson today? Tell me 2 things you did to make it a good lesson.
> What has gone well for you today? What difference has that made?
> 3 good things your friends (or teachers) have noticed about you so far today?

5 minute conversation prompts

> Think about a time when you were at your best (insert area if applicable e.g. in your maths or keeping calm).
> 4 things you were pleased to notice.
> 3 things you did that you are proud of.
> 2 things you learnt about yourself.
> 1 thing you will notice yourself doing more of tomorrow.

28. Using scales

The 0-10 'worst to best' scale structure is the most versatile tool available to build a conversation from a clear beginning to a useful end, by inviting descriptions around three core points:

1. *A description of what success will look like*: for example, 10 could describe 'the student you want to be' or 'a day going well' and 0 the furthest from that you have ever been. When we locate the 0 on a scale as the furthest from the 10 as possible, the more likely it is that some small signs of progress or something helpful to work with will emerge.
2. *A simple way of highlighting progress alongside all that has contributed to this*: 'Which bits of your better day are already happening at your current number?' The emphasis on progress rather than assessing the extent of the problem allows for recognition, even within the lowest of numbers, of all that has been useful as a basis for further progress.
3. *An exploration of signs of progress in the immediate future at one point up on the scale*: 'Suppose tomorrow things were one point higher towards your better day or the student you want to be, what might you and others notice?' or 'What might be the most surprising things you will be telling me about at the end of tomorrow?' The emphasis on several signs helps to reveal potential evidence of progress, whilst at the same time, leaving a supple space for the student to mould in their own way.

Once a scale has been set up, it can be returned to again and again with a freshness born out of the new details to emerge. For example, a student can be periodically asked to reflect on where they would place themselves today or they can be asked to give a number daily over the course of a week. If there is time, they could be asked to discuss the good things, where they would like to be by the end of the week or the following week, what would be the small signs of progress towards this and so on. Over time, these opportunities for students to think about and reflect on will gradually build an image of someone who has skills, qualities and ideas that work for them. Of course, sometimes numbers go down as well as up and sometimes they stay the same. It is important to normalise this pattern of ups and downs as a feature of life and turn the spotlight on the useful behaviours that are *still* evident, whatever the number.

What if someone puts themselves at a 0 on a scale?

In this difficult situation our questions can bring a sense of optimism and a belief that change is possible, whilst at the same time we need to stay close to the student's 0. If our enquiry seems too 'positive' they might not be able to see it.

- *So, it sounds like it's been a hard week. How have you managed to keep going?* Even when there is lack of discernible progress, there are always resources to be gathered.
- *Even though things are not going as you would like them to at the moment, what are you doing to stop things from being even lower on the scale, say -1?* Although this might seem like an odd question, the scale is a guide only and a 'minus number' offers a reference point to pick up on useful behaviours that have kept things going.
- *When were you last above 0? What were you doing then?*
- *What would a 0.5 look like? What will you or your teachers notice tomorrow that will be the tiniest signs that things are back on track?* Keeping the next sign of progress small can make change or progress seem more accessible.
- *How will you know that you are ready to move to a 0.5?* This conveys a confidence that improvement is possible whilst taking into account the pace and style of the individual.

What if someone puts themselves at a 10 on the scale

There will be occasions when a student chooses to put themselves much higher on the scale than anyone else would agree with. A 10 from a student could be the result of many different things: I am not clear enough about the 10; if I say this you might leave me alone; I think I am doing much better than people say I am. The principle would be to see the 10 as an opening rather than an ending to the conversation.

- *Finding out more about the 10*: 'Let's look again at all the things that are happening at your 10' brings actions and ideas into the light. The student might not actually be doing all of these things. Talking about them increases the likelihood that they might go on to do them in the future.
- *Maintaining the 10*: 'How will you know that you are keeping things at your 10 tomorrow?' 'What else would tell you that things are continuing to go well over the next week?' This is a discussion about further progress couched within the 10 the student has offered.
- *Signs of progress*: 'What will an 11 look like?' suggests that we can continue to look and learn. A future focused conversation can then expand on what this would look like, what others would notice and so on.
- *Other persons' perspectives*: If it appears the student is saying '10' as a way to close down the conversation, and we know others (including ourselves) would not agree that they are at 10, then rather than trying to persuade the student that they are wrong, we could introduce the perspective of others. 'What number do you think your teacher would give?' 'What number do you think I would give?' 'What tells them/I that you are at *that* number rather than lower? What would tell them/me you are at +1?' At no point would we say something like: 'So you're not really at 10, are you?!' We accept their number and merely introduce another perspective.

5 minute 'best version' scale

> Let's imagine there is a scale where 10 represents the best version (student you want to be, a good day, etc.) and 0 is the opposite.
> What number represents where you see yourself at the moment? What are you already doing? 5 details
> Suppose later today (tomorrow, this lesson) you had moved up one point, what will be happening? What will you be doing? What else will be different? 4 details
> What will be the tiniest signs that things are moving in the right direction? 3 details

Where will be 'good enough' on the scale?

Sometimes, particularly when progress is slow, we can ask students if there is any point on the scale that would be a good place to have arrived at, as they are on their way to the 10. This allows for a realistic 'well done' for students in their journey while not curtailing an aspiration of what is possible.

'Where will be good enough?' can also accommodate those students who might be happy with a place lower down the scale. If this is the case, then paying attention to attaining and then maintaining this place is more useful than talking about being at a higher point that is of no interest. Let us return to Tyrone, who you will remember from the beginning of the chapter. Having reached the room they were to talk in but having yet to be on the receiving end of any talking, the practitioner decided they needed to do something different.

A line was drawn across a page to represent a broad scale and Tyrone was asked: 'Do you know students in this school who are good all the time, hand in their work and never get into trouble – let's call that a 10 on this scale?' *Yes.* 'And do you know students in this school who never do anything and in fact get excluded – let's call that a 0?' *Yes.* 'And do you know students in the school who judge just how to keep to the right side of the line of acceptability?' *Yes.* Asked which one would best describe him, Tyrone said the last one and indicated a point on the line roughly around a 3.

It was important to enquire whether this was where Tyrone wanted to be. It was. If there had been a negative response, then the practitioner could have asked Tyrone where he would *like* to see himself, or stepped back and built a more detailed picture of the 10 and 0, or enquired how he would know this conversation hadn't been a complete waste of his time (he might, for example, say that it bothers him how others, such as staff, respond to him and be willing to work on that).

Tyrone was then asked what it was about the 3 that fitted well with him and heard how he could be himself *and* not be in too much trouble. He was not interested in being good or toeing the line and did not have many good things to say about the school. However, it was an opening:

- How good are you at staying at this point and not going further down? *It varies.* How do you judge this? How do you manage this? *I see how many times I am asked to speak to someone.*
- Have you ever been any lower? *Yes, but not right to the bottom.*
- What stopped you from skidding right down to the bottom? *I up my game and remind myself that I do not want to be excluded because my mates are here.*
- When you have been lower, how have you managed to get yourself back up again? *I go underground for a couple of weeks.*

As the conversation proceeded, so the length of Tyrone's answers increased and the practitioner was able to pick up and ask more about some of his statements. Given his reticence, the practitioner was selective about which of these to highlight. For example, what did 'going underground' look like? Amongst other things Tyrone stated: 'I don't get into fights, I just walk past trouble'.

At this point, Tyrone was asked about what the school's view of things would be, and if *they* would be ok for him to stay where he was. This is a respectful way to insert the school's view into the conversation. After a pause, Tyrone reflected that a bit higher would probably be better and the rest of the conversation focused on what this would look like from his and the school's points of view. Tyrone returned twice more and the conversations helped him to navigate the choppy waters between his own desires and the requirements of the school. He was not a model pupil, however neither was he excluded.

5 minute conversation prompts to bring in the school's views

> Where do you think I, the school or your teacher would put things?
>
> What good things have we already been noticing? What else?
>
> Is that number ok? Where do you think I, your teacher, the school would want to see things?
>
> What would be different if that was the case?
>
> How would that be good for you?
>
> Suppose things did move to that point, what can we look forward to seeing?

29. Creative scales

Scales can reach beyond numbers to more bespoke versions that are fun to create and use. Most to least favourite foods, music, cartoon characters or whatever the student chooses can all take their place in a 0-10 line up, providing an engaging context with which to discuss how things are going. Mark, a Year 7 student, had created a 'crisps scale' to help him look at how he was managing across the school day. Difference in behaviour for each of the flavours had been considered and recorded. Eventually, Mark would pass his tutor in the corridor with the announcement: 'I am a beef and onion today'. It was an enjoyable interchange that carried with it a wealth of information.

The essence of a scale can also come in many guises. In a Year 1 class, Raul was in constant trouble. The school's behaviour model was a series of rockets that were headed for the Golden Planet. Students moved up and down the coloured rockets according to specific behaviours which were clearly outlined. The teacher wanted to think about how to adapt the system in a way that would help Raul.

The first change was to use the whole length of the rocket rather than simply 'on' or 'off'. Breaking down each rocket into several steps allowed more room to manoeuvre and the opportunity to focus on smaller actions. Raul was hanging onto the back of the bottom rocket, on his own.

The second change was to ask some different questions:

- How come you are hanging on to the back of that rocket? (assumption of intent)
- What are all the things you are doing that are stopping you from falling off? (assumption of competence)
- What will you be doing differently to sit *firmly* on the back of the rocket? (assumption of progress)
- Suppose Blake (his friend who was at the front of the rocket) could reach down and give you a pull up, how would he do that? (building support and motivation)

Although Raul continued to be an 'up and down rocket' student, the teacher found that engaging him in this type of discussion helped him to get back on track more quickly. It is perhaps apposite at this point to recognise the importance of teacher energy in the classroom and the replenishing quality of energising conversations with students.

30. Dealing with challenging conversations

Choosing which bits of an answer to respond to

It is not possible to respond to everything that has been said. We need to make choices about what we pick up on, governed by those details we think will be useful and pertinent to what is wanted.

Take, for example, Amy, a Year 7 student, who was pretty disenchanted with school and talked about the need to improve her behaviour. However, the signs of this, including getting on with her work and not getting into arguments, were fairly standard and not delivered with much enthusiasm. Each of her answers *could* have been pursued for more details. For example, 'Suppose you were not getting into arguments, what would you be doing instead?' The frank question Amy *was* asked: 'Can you do these things?' led to the answer: 'Yes, but I don't try'. A logical question at this point would have been: 'Why don't you try?' but this would in most likelihood have led to further complaints or have firmed up Amy's good reasons for not trying, such as 'the lessons are boring' or 'the teachers don't give me a chance'. An alternative was to point curiosity towards the 'yes' part of Amy's answer: 'You can? How do you know? Give me an example'.

As Amy started to describe what she could do, aided by a number of 'What else?' enquiries, so she started to build a description of herself as someone who got on with her work and avoided arguments. At the end of the discussion, Amy was asked to continue to notice the times when she was trying. A week later, after a short second discussion, the head of year sent an email reporting how Amy had had an 'awesome day today with 10/10 in all her lessons'. She reported Amy had been overheard saying to another student in class: 'It's not that hard to be quiet' and 'It's good to be good'.

What else?

Sometimes persistence in the form of 'What else?' is never more useful than when helping a student move beyond the repetitive or downright unhelpful. It communicates that there is more to find out and also that students do ultimately know what is good for them. A Year 8 student, Nuhu, who had had a very difficult day, was asked how he would know that tomorrow was going better for him. Nuhu responded with: 'The school will have burned down'. This may well have been one thought or hope, but the assumption would be that this was not his *only* thought or hope. There then followed a sequence of 'What else?' questions:

Practitioner:	What else will tell you that tomorrow is going better for you?
Nuhu:	All the teachers would have been sacked.

Practitioner:	And what else will you be noticing?
Nuhu:	I would be so brilliant I would not have to go to lessons.
Practitioner:	Ok. What else?
Nuhu:	I would have friends.

Having friends was a context within which change and difference could reside and thus be worth pursuing by asking questions like: 'What difference will this make?', 'What will this help you to do or do more of?'

What if the student just keeps saying 'don't know?'

Most of us have been on the receiving end of various versions of 'I don't know' or 'I don't care'. However, 'I don't know' can mean a number of different things and be responded to in a number of different ways. We would therefore treat 'I don't know' as an answer, and treat each 'I don't know' as a separate answer. Several ideas have already been outlined in Part 1: Chapter 8 which looks at conversational prompts such as 'have a guess' or utilising the views of others who may have an interest in how things are going.

The following extract is at the beginning of a conversation with a 14-year-old called Karen who has been asked to see the school counsellor. It illustrates how beginning with the end in mind and drawing on the views of friends can help to develop a useful focus for the work.

Counsellor:	What are you best hopes from this meeting?
Karen:	Dunno.
Counsellor:	What will tell you it's been useful?
Karen:	Dunno.
Counsellor:	What are you hoping it will lead to?
Karen:	Dunno.
Counsellor:	How will you know it's not been a waste of your time?
Karen:	Dunno.
Counsellor:	How will your friends know it's not been a waste of time?
Karen:	I won't be so unhappy.
Counsellor:	How would they know that?
Karen:	I would talk to them.
Counsellor:	You would talk to them. What else?
Karen:	I'd focus on my work more.

(from Ratner and Yusuf 2015: 47-48)

What if a student is refusing to speak

The most extreme form of 'don't know' is not saying anything at all. de Shazer referred to three simple rules which he said formed the underlying philosophy of SFP: 'If it ain't broke, don't fix it; if it works, do more of it; and if it doesn't work, don't do it again, do something different' (de Shazer 1989: 93). Here are examples of doing something different to try and open up a doorway into a conversation.

1. Validation

A deputy head teacher had been asked to remove Tom, a Year 4 student, from class following an incident and his subsequent refusal to follow the teacher's instructions. As they were walking down the corridor to her room, Tom had refused to say anything. The deputy head teacher responded by making a simple statement: 'You know, sometimes it is absolutely the right thing to be quiet'. She then started tidying things in her room and asked Tom if he could help. Having taken the pressure off of 'talking about what had happened', the deputy head asked Tom how he had learnt to tidy so well and gradually the conversation turned to what else Tom did in class that was helpful. Finally, she asked Tom if he would like things to go better in class when he returned and what this would look like from his and the teacher's points of view. Tom talked about what he would do and what he would say to the teacher, which included an apology.

2. Talking through another person

A student can be listening and looking even if they are not talking. A slightly quirky approach is to conduct a conversation with an additional person in the presence of the student, whilst at the same time looking for opportunities to invite their views.

  A mentor from the Learning Support Unit was working with Dionne, a Year 10 student teetering on the edge of permanent exclusion following a major fight with another student. However, Dionne was refusing to talk to anybody about the incident. The practitioner asked the mentor to check with Dionne if she would be interested in filming a discussion where they would interview the mentor who would pretend to be Dionne. It was with some surprise that Dionne agreed.

  At the start, Dionne was told that she could interrupt at any time if she felt the mentor was not doing her justice in what she was saying. The practitioner began by asking 'Dionne' about what had happened and what she had found helpful. At one point, Dionne interrupted to correct the mentor on a detail about where the incident had taken place, but apart from that she watched and filmed. 'Dionne' was then asked how she would know that things were moving on in a way that was good for her. At the end of the 10 minute discussion, the practitioner turned to Dionne behind the camera and asked her to state, using a scale, how accurately she felt the conversation had represented how she saw things. Dionne answered with an 8, saying: 'It's pretty much how I feel'. Two significant things changed as a result of this discussion: the mentor felt more confident in how she was approaching things and Dionne felt that she had been understood. They continued to work together and the practitioner had the occasional 10 minute conversation with the mentor to reflect on what was working and how to build on this. At the end of Year 11, just after Dionne's final GCSE exam, the deputy head teacher talked about the school's pride in keeping Dionne in school until she had sat her exams. Five years later, the same member of staff bumped onto Dionne near the school and learnt that she was just about to complete a beautician's course and was looking forward to getting her first salon job.

'It's not fair'

Trying to counter an argument that is a variation on 'it's not fair' or someone else should be doing something often leads to the student finding even more reasons or examples to back their viewpoint. A first step would be to accept and acknowledge without agreeing, for example, 'So from your point of view that sounds unfair' and then look to build a useful conversation.

- *Building interactional descriptions*: Suppose they did do (insert desired behaviour), what difference would it make to you? How would you respond? And if you did that, how might they respond? Alternatively, we can ask the student to imagine that *they* were to do something different and track through the responses that might follow this.
- *Checking the likelihood of change using a scale*: Even a low number forms the basis for exploring this much confidence and how to build on it.
- *Using a 'both/and' framework*: Imagine things do not change *and* you somehow manage to find a way through that is good for you and the school, what will you be noticing?

Mark, a Year 10 student, was at his most animated when talking about his frustrations with his year head 'waiting around the corner to pounce on me and embarrass me in front of my friends'. The veracity of this statement was less important than the motivation it gave Mark to think about what the head of year, in particular, might need to see different in order to stop paying him so much attention, how she might respond and what difference this would make to Mark. Thus, instead of being focused on what Mark thought the head of year should stop doing, it turned into a conversation about what potential change could look like, and from there built a picture of the ripple effect of these changes. A crucial question was to explore how Mark would respond in a way that would support his desire to reduce his visibility should the head of year not immediately notice his efforts.

What if someone is just saying what they think we want to hear?

Every answer or response to a question offers an opening to find out more. Requiring 'harder' thinking on the part of the student can sometimes reveal a commitment they might not know they had.

- *Exploring the benefits*: 'Suppose you did do more of (insert detail). How will this be good for you?'
- *Exploring good reasons*: 'You must have a good reason for saying (insert detail) and I am curious what that is'.

- *Exploring difference*: 'What difference will (insert detail) make to how things go for you in school?'
- *Exploring what it will look like*: Tracking in fine detail how (insert detail) will show in lessons or in corridors, etc.
- *Exploring other perspectives*: 'What would I and others need to see to convince us that you are serious about (insert detail)?'

31. When there has been a set-back

The life of most students who are experiencing difficulties is up and down – sometimes things go better and sometimes they don't. When things have taken a downward turn it is easy to dismiss everything as a failure. However, the totality of this dismissal can sometimes mask a change which has occurred but not been noticed, as in the case of Grace, a Year 8 student. Grace was finding it difficult to get on with anybody in school and there had been several major arguments with both staff and students. During a description of how difficult things had been, Grace mentioned: 'I did try and keep my temper on Monday, but people kept winding me up and I couldn't just walk away'. Rather than writing off Monday, two strands of enquiry were followed:

- Firstly, the thinking she had brought into her life: 'How come you made the decision that you were going to *try* not to lose your temper on Monday?' This validated the fact that Grace had started out with the intention that she wanted to keep her temper.
- Secondly, the small successes she might have had: 'On Monday, did you lose your temper for the whole day or were there bits of the day when you managed to keep your temper?'

Grace recalled that she had chatted with some of her friends at the beginning of the day and had asked her teachers if she could sit at the front of the class so she did not become distracted by little arguments. The Monday that now emerged was a day when students and teachers had, for some of the time, been treated to a different side of Grace, a happier and more content side, a day when she had been more selective about the times she stood up for herself.

If a student does not obviously offer an opening, we can help them by asking more direct questions to guide thinking towards identifying small behaviours often overlooked or forgotten.

- When are the times recently when you have managed to stay calm?

If a student is unable to locate a full-blown instance of in-control behaviour, a useful question is:

- What is the closest you have come to having the control that you want?

Helping a student to locate past or current achievements and notice and name associated qualities, helps them to build a description of themselves that fits with the greater likelihood that they can achieve their goals. As this happens, so the journey towards where they want to be becomes firmer and more hopeful. At the end of the discussion, Grace commented: 'It is good talking. It makes me think about what I am doing. I *can* do things normally and not have to change for others'.

Resilience: 'getting back up again' skills

Whenever students lose their cool, screw up their work in frustration or whatever blow-out they have, the SF approach is to pay attention to:

- how the student got themselves back on task again
- how they calmed themselves down enough to eventually have another go
- how they stopped the frustration from building up even higher or impeding all their learning for the rest of the week.

This moves away from the specifics of an incident, what caused the difficulty and ways to sort this out, towards the more generic framework of 'keeping going'. Taking into account the variability of life's hurdles, this connects the student with their kit bag of skills that can have relevance to whatever crops up. The 'excavation' of these skills brings them into the light so that they can be deliberately called upon rather than just appear according to mood or the weather.

A teacher had set up a traffic light system in her class with Ali, a Year 4 student, where each session was allocated green, red or orange depending on how well it had gone. At the end of each day there was usually a splattering of all three colours. Instead of focusing on the downward turn from green to orange or orange to red, the teacher began to discuss any change in the *upward* direction of red to orange or orange to green and what had helped. What was noticeable was how keen Ali was to seek out the teacher to explain what he had done when he had changed things from 'bad' to 'good'. The more he talked about what he did, the stronger and more available these behaviours became. In this way Ali built an image of himself as an active participant in the life that he wanted rather than the life he didn't want. The teacher also periodically indicated her own colour in order to make more explicit what she was also looking out for and noticing.

Other useful questions when there has been a setback might include:

- Was every bit of your maths lesson difficult, or were there some bits that were a little better? *The intention is not to challenge the student's view of difficulty. However, 'bits' hints that the situation may not be absolute and offers an opening into competence.*
- How have you managed to keep going or do as much as you have done today even though it has been difficult? What have you been pleased to notice? *Validating effort and intention.*

- When you have met this kind of thing before, what have you done that has helped or what else has helped? *Building a history of sorting things out.*
- What are your ways of making mistakes useful? *Assuming competence and offering a different way of looking at mistakes.*
- How will you know you are at your best when you are finding something is difficult? *Looking to future possibilities.*

32. Confidence

How to 'do' confidence

Miriam, a Year 12 student, wanted to be more confident in class, 'but I don't know how to do it'. In her own way, Miriam recognised that unless there are observable actions that can be seen or experienced, confidence can remain an elusive quality. When a student becomes separated from a sense of possibility in themselves, it is natural to want to bolster them by pointing out any good things they have done. However, this could create the impression that we don't fully understand the difficulties, which in turn, can lead to the student telling us more about them. As we help students *themselves* to locate concrete and detailed indicators of what confidence, self-belief or whatever would look like in their lives, the more likely it is to make a lasting difference. There are a number of possible routes that can start this search – any or all will be helpful:

- Route 1: How will this confidence show?
- Route 2: What difference will this confidence make?
- Route 3: If you woke up tomorrow to discover you have all the confidence you need, what might be the very first sign that would tell you this?
- Route 4: What will others notice that will tell them that your confidence is growing?
- Route 5: How will you know that others have noticed your increased confidence and what will you do in response?

Miriam was taken via 'route 3' and asked to detail what a video camera would be picking up as her day unfolded. The following is an extract from the discussion which illustrates how tracking one idea can help to reveal a number of other useful pointers.

Practitioner:	What else would be a sign of the 'confident you' tomorrow?
Miriam:	Not rushing and trying to do lots of things at the same time.
Practitioner:	Hmm. So if you were not rushing and trying to do lots of things at the same time, what will you be doing instead?
Miriam:	Well ... I don't know ... . Probably concentrating on one thing.
Practitioner:	Ok. And how would this show? No – maybe a better question is, what difference would that make?
Miriam:	I would spend more time on things.

Practitioner:	Ah. I see. And what, for you, would be a sign of spending more time on things? It's important to know what things would look like from your point of view.
Miriam:	Well, if I was doing that, I would probably spend more time on thinking and planning.
Practitioner:	That's interesting. And what would you notice about the way you were planning?
Miriam:	I would be really thinking about what I had to do. Just thinking about that and not everything all at once.

As the conversation continued, Miriam's description of her confidence included more and more details about how this would show in the way she organised herself. A fortnight later, Miriam sat down and produced a colourful pad in which she had been writing notes to herself, jotting down questions she could ask and even making small schedules. This had made a huge difference to her in keeping better track of what was being said in class and gave her something to work from outside of the lesson. Change is progressive and so we will listen out for and amplify those changes that will help this progression along, for example:

- What did you notice yourself doing at this point? How was that good for you? What else?
- What did your teachers notice when you did that? How did they respond?
- How will you know that these skills are getting stronger? What will you, your teachers, your friends notice?

Miriam did not need another session. Her teachers reported that she was happier, more focused and contributing more in class. She had told them:

> Our discussion made me think more about the effort I am making. I was only thinking of how much I was failing. I felt more positive and focused after our discussion and this made me notice the small successes. Doing these things has shown me that I can be confident and do things.
>
> (Miriam)

Younger students could be asked to show what confidence looks like. For example, Year 5 and 6 students were asked to work in groups. Through a series of plays, raps, dances and poetry they demonstrated what confidence meant to them. The discussions that accompanied these 'performances' helped to solidify the finer points of confidence in action.

Confidence scales

When a student has detailed what they want for themselves, another possibility is to then explore their confidence in *achieving* this outcome or *continuing* to make progress. In this way, confidence would not be treated as an outcome in itself, but a valuable support to a student in taking the steps they want to take.

So we might enquire: On a scale of 0–10 with 10 standing for you having every confidence that you will indeed achieve or make progress towards the best hopes you have for yourself, and 0 standing for the opposite, where would you put your confidence today?

Alternatively, the student can be asked how confident they are of reaching the good-enough point they had assigned on their overall scale.

- The student can be invited into listing all the reasons to be as confident as they are.
- In addition to what they know about themselves, we can also ask what others might know about them. 'What does your mum, teacher or best friend see in you that would support your confidence of 4?' will reveal yet more useful skills and resources. It is also possible to enquire as to how much confidence others have in them to make progress – students sometimes recognise that their friends (for example) have even more belief in them than they have themselves, and it can be useful to explore what gives them that belief.
- It is also possible to look to the past for inspiration, for example, 'When has your confidence been at its highest in the past in relation to (insert best hopes)?'
- If the number is low, it is useful to locate even smaller signs of progress on the outcome scale before exploring the student's confidence in achieving this.
- Additionally, we can explore how the student will know that their confidence had moved just one point up. A Year 4 student, Talia, said that reading every day with Audrey in the upstairs flat would increase her confidence in her reading. Once identified, this was set up and made a big difference to Talia, with the added confidence boost of having come up with the idea herself.

33. Motivation

Students of most ages will talk about times when they are not 'in the mood' for studying or just can't settle to their work in class. Viewed as an enormous barrier to doing what they know they should be doing, it closes down imagination and effort. We would seek to normalise a fluctuation in concentration and then help students to move beyond the all or nothing of 'being in the mood' for working.

'Being bothered' scales

Valuing and strengthening effort can have an impact on outcomes. So when a conversation feels like walking through treacle, one approach is to find out from the student their level of motivation. Tone and genuine curiosity are essential ingredients when asking the following:

- How important is it to you for things to improve, with, say, 10 equals this is the most important thing in your life right now?
- How much are you going to put in to help things improve, let's say 10 equals you'll do anything, even walk on hot coals in bare feet?

Whatever the number given, we can explore, in a similar way to the confidence scale above, the foundations for their current number and what moving up the scale would lead to.

'Both-and' rather than 'either-or'

A 'both-and' question seeks to bring together two seemingly polarised standpoints and open a third way that can accommodate them both:

- Can you think about a time when you were not in the mood for studying *and* managed to get some work done?

Alternatively, we can ask:

- What is the *closest* you have come to doing your work over these last few weeks, even though it has been hard?

Exploring all that was happening at that time might reveal something that can be built on. Even a statement such as: 'I only managed to do all my work in class once this week', contains a productive part – 'managed once' – that can be further explored.

Future focus

'Let's imagine for a moment that tomorrow is a day when you *are* going to be able to get down to your work. Although it might seem unlikely, just imagine for a moment that it was possible. What would be the first thing you would notice that would give you a clue tomorrow that this was the case?' Ideas can come from the most surprising places and our questions can help to make the invisible more visible.

Rob, a Year 11 student, was finding it difficult to get on with his work at the weekend. He spent some time describing how he would try and fail. Rob was first asked to imagine that next Saturday was a day when he would be able to get down to his work. Starting from the moment he got up, what would he notice that would be different? At this point, Rob explained that he played rugby for a team on Saturday mornings and how he would get up and immediately put on his rugby kit. Asked what difference this made, Rob described how it helped him to 'get in the zone'. SF dialogues are built in the moment, drawing on what has been said to formulate the next question. So taking Rob's phrase about 'being in the zone', the practitioner was then curious what signs he would notice on Saturday that tell him he was 'in the zone' for getting down to his work. Rob replied 'shoes'.

However bizarre an idea might seem, it is worth pursuing to see where it leads. So Rob was asked what he would notice about the way he was putting on his shoes that would tell him that he was 'in the zone' for working. Slowing down descriptions and focusing on the smallest elements can make the difference between a glimpse and a full-on look at an idea. Rob in fact answered the question in a different way: that putting his shoes on would give him a sense of being ready, like he meant business. Again, taking a lead from Rob's answer, the practitioner continued to explore how else he would know that he meant business. It is unlikely that 'shoes' would appear on any tip list for studying. However, its bespoke nature made it an accessible and effective basis for a solution for Rob.

Getting going

A student once asked YA how *she* got herself going when she was finding it difficult. As someone who hates ironing, the most effective method for YA is to lay out the board, iron and clothes ready, and then return later. 'Ironing board' ideas from students have included getting out all their books and materials in advance; noting down three bullet points on a page before stopping a piece of work so there is something to come back to; or finding an easy task to start with.

34. Anxiety

Doing yourself justice in exams

There are students who can function in the school environment but who find it almost impossible to perform in a formal test setting. The visualisation and experiential nature of the SF 'At your best' or 'Doing yourself justice' frameworks can be key in creating an alternative story with students about themselves in relation to the exam process, one where they own the narrative through the identification of many potential indicators.

The following is a 10 minute discussion with a Year 11 student called Sadiq who was panicking about taking his exams. He is sitting with his friend Hamid. We track through the morning of his first exam.

Practitioner:	Right. I am going to ask you a slightly unusual question. Is that ok?
Sadiq:	Yes.
Practitioner:	Let's imagine that it is Wednesday, the day of your maths exam. You wake up in the morning and it is a day when you are going to be at your best in your exam. What is the first thing you will notice?
Sadiq:	I would wake up worrying and feeling sick.
Practitioner:	Ok. Let's imagine it is next Wednesday and, despite your worrying and feeling sick, you are at your best. What is the first thing you would notice that would give you a hint about this?
Sadiq:	I would wake up and not be thinking I can't do it.
Practitioner:	What would you be thinking instead? If the thoughts about 'I can't do it' have gone, what will be taking their place?
Sadiq:	That I can do it.
Practitioner:	Ok. Can I ask you a bit more about this?
Sadiq:	Yes.
Practitioner:	What in particular would you be thinking about this? That you can do it?
	Hmm. I would be thinking ... hmm. I would be thinking about some of the things that I know I can do in the subject.

Practitioner:	Ah. I see. Thinking about the things that you know you can do. And what would be the next sign of you at your best as you are getting ready?
Sadiq:	I will have more time.
Practitioner:	How come?
Sadiq:	I won't be trying to look up last minute things.
Practitioner:	That's interesting. What will you be doing instead?
Sadiq:	I will be able to take my time and do things slower.
Practitioner:	And what difference would this make? Taking things slower?
Sadiq:	Hmm. I would feel calmer.

Sadiq goes on to describe how his mother and sister would notice that he was in a good mood, and that he might even talk to his sister about something on YouTube, which would help him to feel more composed. As he leaves the house he will be walking with a sense of purpose and maybe even feel a little excited.

Practitioner:	Who might you meet up with on your way to school?
Sadiq:	Someone who I can go through the questions with.
Practitioner:	Who is a good person to do this with?
Sadiq:	Only those students who are smart and helpful! (*indicates his friend sitting next to him*)
Practitioner:	How will you know they are smart and helpful?
Sadiq:	Well, they wouldn't be saying they can't do it or what they are worried about.
Practitioner:	Ok. So what would be happening with these smart and helpful students instead?
Sadiq:	Hmm. We might be going through difficult questions or topics and getting ideas from each other.
Practitioner:	And then let's imagine you have now arrived at the school. What would you notice about how you were still at your best this morning?
Sadiq:	Definitely not going with the crowds. I would choose either to be first or last into the hall.
Practitioner:	That's interesting. What difference would this make?
Sadiq:	I won't get caught up in unhelpful conversations. I can just go in and settle down and start thinking.

As he entered the hall, Sadiq would be telling himself to calm down and that he had the knowledge, whatever they asked. If the exam started with a difficult question, he would jot down some ideas and then do an easier question to get himself going. These may well have been thoughts Sadiq already had, but viewed within the context of 'being at his best' they held a different meaning for him.

At the end of the conversation Sadiq and Hamid went straight to find their head of year. They asked if they could go and talk with the Year 10 students as they thought it would be very helpful to them to think in this way.

Looking back from beyond

When there is something difficult coming up, it can be useful to leapfrog, as it were, over the event and to build a picture from a successful point beyond it. The slightly unusual nature of the question can release students from focusing on things that are difficult and dip into the more creative and hopeful part of their thinking.

Hayley was a Year 11 student who was extremely anxious about the GCSE exams. She stated clearly that she did not think a discussion could in any way help her. However, the fact that Hayley had come, and was staying in the room, encouraged the practitioner to persist with some questions.

Practitioner:	Can I ask a different question?
Hayley:	If you want.
Practitioner:	Imagine it is the end of the year and you have just done your last GCSE exam. Although you don't know what the results are yet, you feel a sense of achievement with what you have done, how you went about your studying and the way you handled the difficulties. Looking back over the year, what will you be remembering?
Hayley:	I came to see a counsellor *(said with heavy irony)*.
Practitioner:	And what happened at the counselling that turned out to be useful for you?
Hayley:	The counsellor asked lots of questions *(more irony and eyes rolling to the ceiling)*.
Practitioner:	And what difference did those questions make?
Hayley:	I don't know *('don't know' rarely means the student doesn't know anything. I treated this as the fact that she needed more time to think)*.
Practitioner:	What do you reckon?
Hayley:	They helped me to think.
Practitioner:	Ok. And what difference did this thinking make?
Hayley:	It helped me remember what was good for me.

We went on to list all the things she would have done that would have been good for her.

Increasing options and control

When serious issues to do with anxiety (and related behaviours, including self-harm) come to light, the safety of the students is, of course, the top priority and the situation needs to be carefully monitored and followed up. In some cases, there will be a need to talk to the student and their parents about getting help from their GP and possibly a referral to a specialist service such as CAMHS.

When a conversation is appropriate, an important focus is on increasing the options the student has for dealing with stress so that their sense of control builds up over time. Each student is unique and amplifying their particular approach validates thought and action. For example, at a meeting with Corrie and his mother, Corrie outlined his strategies for containing his panic attacks, including alerting the teacher to the need to let him sit quietly in another room for a few minutes. As the work together continued, his need to draw on these strategies lessened until they were no longer needed. Skye, a young woman in Year 9, said that her techniques for dealing with her anxiety included taking deep breaths, writing down her dark thoughts and then throwing the paper away and using a mindfulness app. She had made considerable progress by the time of the second meeting and so the practitioner asked her what advice she would have for students with the same issue. Skye said she would tell them to ignore it, use the 'write and throw' method and talk to someone to 'get it out'. The practitioner asked her where the 'write it down and throw it away' idea had come from and she said that she had talked to another girl who had made the suggestion!

In addition to the more problem-solving aspects of the above illustrations, we would also look for opportunities to focus on what difference 'managing your anxiety' or 'having no anxiety' would make to the student's *life*. We assume that if someone has a sense of their preferred future, the preferred outcome of what they are trying to deal with, then this will stimulate and support their efforts, strength and belief in moving forward. The practitioner was asked to speak with Sarah who was adamant that she did not want to access medical services as she did not want to be prescribed medication for her intense anxiety. She was putting tremendous effort into getting herself into school as often as she could, but she rarely ventured outside her home otherwise. The conversation explored what would be different in her life when the anxiety lessened, who the significant people were in her life and what they would notice, and then using a scale, how far she felt she had come and how she had managed that. In subsequent meetings, the scale was revisited, looking at how she was coping and the small but significant steps she was taking to move forward in her life. On one occasion when there was a setback (Sarah called it a 'relapse'), a conversation was arranged with Sarah and her mother to consider whether she should now go to the doctor, which she still rejected. Overall, it was a slow process, but Sarah made sufficient progress to be able to advance her studies and her social life.

35. Giving advice

Students giving themselves their own advice

When students come to us asking for advice, a pragmatic or expedient approach is to provide them with tips or techniques or signpost them to online resources. If there is time, however, then the situation can also be used as a potential learning opportunity to help the student to develop their own skills and grow.

A group of Year 12 and 13 students wanted help in how they could go about revising. Rather than look at revision as one activity, the students were asked to consider:

- How they revised topics they felt confident about to ensure they kept the knowledge in their mind.
- What they did to increase their understanding and learning in topics they partially knew.

- When knowledge and understanding were very blurred, what they noticed about how they went about helping themselves. How did they know what questions to ask and of whom?

The notion of flexibility is often a revelation to those students who adopt a one size fits all approach and makes space for more creative, bespoke and practical approaches to be shaped. Most students find that when they have a sense of control over content and method, it gives them a different perspective on what they do. As one student commented, although her teacher had been really helpful in giving her ideas, she had found that by viewing topics in terms of how well she knew them helped her to see better how she could begin to make use of the array of revision approaches and techniques on offer.

What if we have a good piece of advice?

On those occasions when we feel we want to give advice *and* we sense the student might be willing to make use of our ideas, we would also ask supplementary questions to encourage the student to find their own unique way of doing that.

- How will you know that this is useful for you?
- Which bits of this might be useful to you? And how will you know?
- How would this fit in with your way of doing things?

The practitioner asked to have a quick chat with Evie, a Year 6 student, who was in constant trouble for talking in class. She had been told that she should just ignore the other students on her table, but Evie did not think she could easily do this. Rather than dismiss the idea in its entirety, Evie was asked if there were any bits of this idea that might be useful to her. She thought for a long while before deciding that saying 'shush' and then looking at her book might work. A week later, Evie proudly talked about getting her best ever mark in her spelling test (19/20). She commented: 'It's hard not talking in class. But last week I tried that thing we talked about. I just said to the people "shush" and then looked back and got on with my work. I have been practicing this at home'.

This could have been left at 'well done'. However, there was also the opportunity to create a dialogue in which the success behind the spelling could express itself again in the future. The practitioner asked Evie what difference it had made to her to ignore other students. Evie stated that by not chatting, she had listened more to her teacher and by listening to him, she had found she could do much more than she thought she could. Evie's teacher commented that she was much more settled in class and talking about her learning in a completely different way.

Similarly, if students talk about something *others* have done that was helpful for them, we can still centralise their agency by enquiring what *they* then did to make use of this support: 'How did you get that to work for you?' The more students understand their own role in shaping ideas, the more independence and confidence this will foster.

36. The enquiring mind: facilitating peer conversations

Learning is as much about what we ask as what we answer. In the context of the busy classroom, providing opportunities for students to build their confidence and competence in asking good questions can support their own learning, stretch the thinking and practice of their peers and generate excitement and energy.

There are many examples of short conversation structures in Part 2 that can be used to structure constructive dialogues between students. Allocating the role of 'journalist' emphasises a question asking rather than an advice giving role. Providing a variety of prepared questions on tables that students can pick out and ask each other encourages experimentation. Students in a Year 6 class were given many opportunities to try out detailing questions when working in pairs. Over time, they became adept at independently building on the answers of others and it was not uncommon to hear a student validate a contribution – 'I like that idea' – followed by: 'Can I just ask you how you will know that this is working?' or 'What would that look like?' Their natural curiosity was supported by an increasing lexicon of useful questions that helped to extend the ideas and perspectives of their peers.

Role playing a sample conversation at the front of the class allows students to see the questions in action. Students can be asked to comment on the interviewer's skills, and to highlight the questions they had liked or thought had worked well in helping the student being interviewed to think.

Here is a 5 minute conversation between two Year 5 students, Claire and May. Both have experienced great difficulty in settling to their learning in class and building relationships with other students. This is the first time that they have worked together and the first time they have explored a SF way of talking. They have been given an initial schedule of questions structured around a scale. As the interview continues, we can see how the interviewer, Claire, begins to experiment with her own ideas. It can often be observed when watching students interviewing each other that they have absolutely no doubt in their peers' capacity to come up with good answers and good ideas.

Claire:	You are trying to …
May:	Do my work independently.
Claire:	Thinking about the scale, where would you put yourself on the scale?
May:	I would put myself on a 5.
Claire:	Why?
May:	Because sometimes I work by myself and sometimes I still ask people for help so I am kind of in the middle.
Claire:	Where did you rate yourself at the beginning?
May:	I rated myself on a 3.
Claire:	How does that show that you are improving?
May:	I am focusing on my work and I am not chatting to other people.
Claire:	How do you see that our teachers are knowing that you are improving?
May:	When I am looking in my book – sometimes I see that I have got everything right and sometimes I see that I got some things wrong.
Claire:	Tell me something else that you are pleased about.

May:	I am pleased that – normally when I go home I just play – but now I start to do work at home as well.
Claire:	How does that show?
May:	Well it shows because my mum was telling me that 'you are really getting smart now'.
Claire:	What difference does it make?
May:	Sometimes when I want to do something, like when my cousins are around, I am not embarrassed because sometimes when I get it wrong they laugh at me and now when I get it right they don't.
Claire:	Tell me other things that you have done that made you say you're at number 5?
May:	When I get up, so say if there is still time before I go to school, I do work and I don't watch TV.
Claire:	Can I ask something myself?
May:	Yes.
Claire:	While you have been in school and at home – because you have a little brother – if you are going to do chores and homework – and if you do something exciting like go to the park – would you do your homework first or go straight away?
May:	I think that I would still go to the exciting place first because I can do my homework after, so it is not really that big a deal if I just go first or after.
Claire:	Sometimes if you do your homework and if you go to the exciting place, what if you lose your focus when you go?
May:	I would – well if I lose my focus I would just remember what my mum told me – I asked her – and she said that I am really independent now, so when I lose my focus – I am trying to get independent by myself. It will help me in the future because say if I wanted to get into college and I was doing a test – I won't be stuck – I will just be rushing through the work and I won't be asking people for help.
Claire:	So, thank you very much. This is the end of the interview.

This might seem like an abrupt ending. However, we tend to remember those parts of a conversation that are of most interest to us and May was left with the freedom to decide which these would be. Claire and May went on to become Learning Ambassadors working with children from a Year 3 class, something that would not have been considered possible for them at the beginning of the school year. They took their role very seriously, often preparing materials at home to use in their sessions. Back in their own classroom their attitude towards their own work and towards other students also became more settled and many ideas about independence found their way into the work of both of them.

These conversations have helped the students to understand they have choices, and the students responded well to a pace that was dictated by them. It was like taking the students on a journey where there were some things laid down about where they were heading, but they can have a say in how they want that journey to be. I am seeing how scale questions can relate to other parts of the curriculum such as topics and English work. The open-ended nature of the questions aids discussion and debate. It has also helped the children to really listen and build on answers. I feel that they have become very good listeners through asking questions.

(Naureen Akhtar, class teacher)

37. Differing 5 minute conversation frameworks around a specific issue

The following represents three different ways 5 minutes could be used around a specific issue, in this case a student wanting to remain calm and be in control of their temper. Each example draws on a different SF framework.

5 minutes: building a picture of what being in control of temper would look like

> So – you would like to be more in control of your temper. Is that right?
> *Yes*
> Let's suppose tomorrow you find that you are in control of your temper. How will you know? What will you notice? What else will tell you? What else x5
> What difference will it make? What else x5
> In what way will it be good for you? What else x5
> Who will notice and what will they see? What else x5
> What will be the first 3 tiny signs tomorrow that you are more in control of your temper?

5 minutes: finding out what the student already knows how to do in terms of temper control

> So – you would like to be more in control of your temper. Is that right?
> *Yes*
> When was the last time that you felt provoked and you didn't lose it? Tell me about it.
> Were you pleased with that?
> How difficult was it for you to handle the situation in the way that you did?
> How did you do it? What else did you do that helped? What else x5
> What did it take for you to do that? What did you draw on – what strengths and skills and resources? What else x5
> How will you know that these things are getting stronger? What else x4

5 minutes: using a scale to locate current successes and future possibilities

> So – you would like to be more in control of your temper. Is that right?
>
> *Yes*
>
> On a scale of 0-10 with 0 standing for the temper is in charge of you and 10 standing for you are in charge of the temper, where do you see things?
>
> How come there and not 0? What else x5
>
> How will you know that you have moved one point higher? What will be small signs of that happening? What else x5
>
> Who else will notice and what will they notice? What else x5
>
> How will you know they have noticed and what effect will this have on you?

References

de Shazer, S. (1990) What is it about Brief Therapy that Works? In Z.J.K and S.G. Gilligan (Eds.) *Brief Therapy: Myths, Methods, and Metaphors*. New York: Brunner/Mazel.

Ratner, H., George, E., and Iveson, C. (2012) *Solution Focused Brief Therapy: 100 Key Points and Techniques*. London: Routledge.

Ratner, H. and Yusuf, D. (2015) *Brief Coaching with Children and Young People: A Solution Focused Approach*. London: Routledge.

Part 4   Coaching, consultations and meetings

Coaching conversations with staff

38. Key considerations

Coaching conversations provide the opportunity to co-create a context for change so that people have an increased sense of purpose and belief. Rather than being viewed as a totally segregated activity, coaching conversations would ideally build on the reflective practice already present in the culture of the school. The SF structure can support the efficiency and effectiveness of these precious allocations of time in building the competence, confidence and expertise of school staff. The focus on building a discourse around outcomes and skills can be used across the full spectrum of peer conversations, on-going professional development and more targeted support for staff. For ease, the term 'coach' will sometimes be used to describe the staff member who is facilitating these conversations.

Practical things to bear in mind

- Coaching conversations in school often have to be fitted around a multitude of other tasks. Whether 2 or 20 minutes is available, what is a constant is the need to be clear about the hoped-for destination of the discussion. This helps to shape the questions and concentrate attention on those things that are most pertinent.
- A supportive structure that includes on-going reflections between sessions will help to encourage staff to notice and attach significance to key developments and support progress over time. An example might involve having an initial 15 minute conversation to establish key areas to work on and what success would look like. Over the next few weeks, the coach could find a couple of moments during each school day to enquire about something the member of staff has been pleased to notice, or to feedback an observation they might have made. A second 15 minute coaching conversation can explore what's been better in more depth and highlight further small signs of progress to look out for.

39. Focusing on what is wanted

The most important place to start

All SF coaching sessions start with asking about the best hopes to establish what the member of staff is wanting to achieve.

- What are your best hopes from our conversations together?
- What are you hoping the coaching will lead to?

In asking these questions we are not attempting to understand the problem, rather to facilitate an articulation of the preferred outcome the member of staff would like to be moving towards. The rest of the conversation will then focus on a detailed description of the presence of this desired outcome and all the things currently residing in the situation that can be amplified or built on to support progress towards this.

The 'best version'

Focusing on the 'best version possible' generates descriptions of potential and effective futures.

- 'Imagine you are at your best tomorrow (or over the next week), at work or in your classroom, what will you notice?'
- Use a scale where 10 denotes 'the teacher (or practitioner) you aspire to be'.
- 'Let's imagine your next lesson with this class turns out to be a good one, what evidence will you be picking up on?'

Each answer given provides the opportunity to search out more detail through questions such as: 'How will that show?' 'What else will be happening?' or 'How will you know this is useful?'

   These questions can be adapted when a specific issue has emerged:

- How will you know that you are on top form in this challenging classroom tomorrow, despite your concerns?
- What would your best work look like in helping the students work more collaboratively in this project?
- What will the students notice about how you are following up on assignments that will communicate your expectations?
- What will tell you that your use of pace and variety is improving in your next lesson with 9T?

Scaling progress

In its simplest form, scales are an efficient way of making space for successes to be examined and progress described in relation to the 'best version'.

- The 10 on the scale represents what success will look like, the best hopes realised. The 0 is usually represented as a statement such as 'the complete opposite', as talking about the 0 is, in effect, focusing on what is not wanted. Without these clear 10 and 0 definitions the answer to the question 'What number would currently describe where things are?' has little meaning.
- Any number except 0 indicates that the journey towards the 10 has already started and provides an opening into what is already working. Eliciting many details about useful behaviours, actions and thoughts validates initiatives and provides many possibilities to build on.
- Further signs of progress can be accessed by describing what would be different one point up the scale. 'Suppose things moved to a 4 on your scale, what will you and others be noticing?' 'What else? What else?' Locating many options increases the feasibility that change will occur.

A coach was asked to work with a struggling student teacher to help him build his confidence and competence in the classroom. As an experienced teacher, the coach had many ideas about classrooms, students, learning and behaviour which she could have shared. However, she decided to start by asking the student teacher himself to describe a good lesson where he and the students were at their best. His initial ideas were often couched in terms such as: 'The students would not be calling out'. 'There wouldn't be so many arguments'. Asking 'What would be happening instead?' or 'What would you be seeing more of instead?' encouraged the teacher to define in more concrete terms what it was that he wanted and thus achieve a clarity about what he could begin to work towards.

The coach then introduced a scale where the best lesson description became the 10 and the 0 was the worst possible lesson. The first part of the conversation looked at all the things 'going right' in the classroom that would support the student teacher's 4 on the scale: 'Tell me about the good things you are already noticing?' 'What else is happening?' 'What have you been doing that has helped bring these things about?' Starting out as a teacher is not an easy thing, so spending time on current successes (or even partial successes) and emphasising the teacher's agency was an important part of a process that sought to build confidence. Finally, the conversation turned to the small differences the student teacher and others (the students, the coach) would notice at one point up the scale.

The scale was periodically returned to over the next couple of weeks, following the same format of examining the successes and highlighting small signs of progress. After several of these scale conversations, the student teacher observed: 'I know you are going to ask me how I think things are going using the scale. So, it makes me look harder for the facts to back up the number I give'. Many things happen in a busy classroom. The scale discussions had encouraged the student teacher to focus on those details most pertinent to building the classroom that he wanted.

At the end of term, the coach reflected on her own SF journey. Asking SF questions had enabled her to step back and help the teacher become his own expert in the classroom. She had been surprised at the number of details simply asking 'What else?' had uncovered. The concrete and specific nature of these details had helped her to feel confident, in her role of supporting good practice, that the student teacher was on track. The scale had also provided a collaborative context within which she was able to occasionally offer her own views of what she had observed going well or what she might also be noticing different at one point up.

40. Amplifying current successes and future opportunities

Using a skills audit

Starting from a base of competence provides a gentle and affirming start to any conversation or piece of work. Once we start paying attention to what is happening at *these* times, we start to reveal potentially useful aspects of behaviour and thought that could become the basis for future change.

In a secondary school the deputy head teacher requested training for a cohort of teacher 'behaviour champions' who would be supporting individual staff around changes they wanted to make in their classrooms. These behaviour champions were all considered to be excellent classroom practitioners and it was hoped they would be able to use their skills and expertise to support others. As an introductory exercise in the first training session, the behaviour champions were asked to work in pairs and take turns to consider:

- 20 skills, qualities and strategies they each brought to their own class teaching.
- The lists were then evaluated to locate the most effective and easiest to do elements.
- Each of *these* elements was then explored further: 'What does that look like?' 'What difference does it make?'

At the end of the exercise, the behaviour champions fed back how interesting it had been to take time to reflect on what they did and how they did it. They had also enjoyed learning about the strengths and approaches of their colleagues. More significantly, at the beginning of the second training session a week later, every one of them commented that making their practice more visible and accessible had made a difference back in their own classrooms. As a consequence, they felt it was something from which all teachers would benefit. They subsequently led an experiential session with the whole staff group in which pairs of teachers interviewed each other using the '20 skills and qualities' framework.

Supporting other teachers

During the course of the training, the behaviour champions developed a clear structure to use in their work with colleagues. They would start by asking the teachers what their best hopes were from the coaching, how they would know it had been useful. They would then use one or more of the following:

- *Building a preferred future description*: How will you know that (insert idea) is becoming stronger and more effective in your work with this class? What might you and the students be picking up on? What will be the first small signs of progress?
- *Amplifying success*: List 15 things that have already gone well in relation to (insert idea). How did you do that? What difference did it make?

- *Building on success*: On the basis of what you have learned, what else will you be pleased to notice over the next week that would tell you these students are (insert idea)? What else will be giving you a sense of pride in your classroom?

The behaviour champions reported that having a structured base of questions increased their own confidence in guiding discussions. Highlighting stronger aspects of practice had also helped to build a rapport with staff members, even those who were less open to asking for help. They liked the respect this approach afforded the teacher's own style and felt that, because the discussed changes were a much better fit, they were more likely to be utilised.

41. A 5 minute coaching conversation

Whether 5 or 50 minutes is available, the most effective consultations create a space for difference to emerge by shaping questions to build a bespoke conversation that is uniquely relevant to *that* member of staff with *that* student, *that* parent, *that* colleague, *that* class or *that* situation. For every question we ask, and every answer we hear, there are a myriad of responses that could be made. However, there are a number of principles which guide practice and it is hoped that the following conversation-with-comments will be helpful in looking 'behind the scenes' at a SF coaching consultation. This discussion with a reception class teacher took place in a morning break.

> Teacher: I want to talk with you about a 5-year-old boy. He has recently come from another school. There was a difficult situation where we had to contact social services because of concerns about some marks on his body. So, the mother is not too happy at the moment. In school, he is bright but aggressive towards other children for no reason. Nothing I have done seems to have had any impact on him. For example, we looked at the 'golden rules' and he was made one of the 'golden rules superheroes'. He had to help other children with the rules but it didn't help.

There is a lot of information here and many strands that could be pursued. We only have the length of the morning break and therefore I need to keep things simple and direct. Bearing in mind that the teacher doesn't want this situation to continue, further forensic analysis of what she doesn't want would not seem to be the best way to use the time.

> Practitioner: So, what are your best hopes from this discussion?

I am searching for a direction for the conversation. Once established, it will provide support for the rest of the discussion and a foundation from which ideas can flow. Other variations could include:
Generic: How will you know this conversation has been useful?

Small, specific: What are the minimum changes that you would want to see to fuel your hope that change is at least possible, however far away it seems at the moment?

> Teacher: Well, ideas about what I can do because I have tried everything and noth-ing has worked.

The first thing to bear in mind is that the teacher has put a lot of thought and effort into her work with this little boy. The second is that it is still not clear what changes the teacher is looking for. Until this is established, any suggestion would be 'free floating', based largely on what might be helpful but with no anchor.

> Practitioner: Ok. So, given what you have told me, and how difficult things are at the moment, what would be the first sign of progress?

'How difficult things are at the moment': Bill O'Hanlon has said we should 'acknowledge AND keep the possibilities open' (O'Hanlon and Beadle 1994: 17). Here an acknowledgment of what has been said about the problem sits alongside maintaining a focus on a hoped-for future. However, asking for 'first signs' introduces a slightly different emphasis in the question. Sometimes it can be easier to focus on little differences when it is hard to imagine things changing.

> Teacher: Well, hitting less.
> Practitioner: Ok. Hitting less. And if he was hitting less, what would he be doing more of?

An essential skill in SFP is to enquire what would take the place of a problem.

> Teacher: Not hitting. *(pause)* Well, sharing more and more calm and friendly behaviour. The thing is he *can* share, because when he sees me look-ing at him, he will share – but in a very exaggerated way. So, he knows how to do it.
> Practitioner: Ok. So, what you are noticing is that he has the skills to be able to share with other students, but he is not using them unless he is being watched.
> Teacher: Yes.

The teacher not only has ideas about what she would like to see, she has also observed them happening (although not quite in the way she would like). By checking out that I have heard correctly, the intention is to stay close to what the teacher is saying. Repetition can also give time for the coach to formulate what they want to ask next. Having introduced the notion of the student having 'sharing skills', one choice could be to explore further evidence for these skills ('Suppose he were to get better at sharing, how would this show?'). However, by continuing to keep the initial questions broad, it is hoped to encourage a wider vista from which many paths can open up. Narrowing down onto too specific a 'target' at this stage can shade potentially useful ideas from view.

Practitioner:	And if he was using these skills more and sharing more, what difference would that make?
Teacher:	He would be getting on better with other children and doing things more with them. Take this morning. There was an activity around the white board where he was in a group and each child had to come and write something on the board. All the children were waiting their turn, but he was very disruptive – grabbing their pens – and he made it very difficult to carry on with the activity.

The teacher's response again opens up a choice about what to follow up. One possibility would be to enquire how the teacher managed to 'keep going' (a coping question) with the activity despite the disruptions. However, there is also the possibility to return to the future, again with a slight change in emphasis.

Practitioner:	Hmm. So, if we were to look at this activity right from the beginning, at its best, what would be happening at the start?
Teacher:	Listening to instructions.
Practitioner:	And what would be the next bit?

The teacher can now 'see' this and moves seamlessly into the description of what it is that she is wanting. The discussion continued until there was a sequential description of activities: listening to instructions, getting the pens out, talking together about which order the students would be standing in to get their turn, and listening to what each other had to say.

Practitioner:	Let's take, for example, negotiating the order. If this were to be broken down into smaller skills and actions, what would be happening?
Teacher:	Talking together about who will go first and then getting the right order in the line. Actually, this is very interesting, because now I'm thinking, when he was asked about the 'golden rules', he just said 'don't' for all the things. And what we are talking about is the 'do'. I need to help him think about what you do – and make it visual. And look at the small bits of what you do for each of the bigger bits. He probably doesn't know that.
Practitioner:	And that lovely idea you had about him being the 'golden rules superhero'. I wonder if there was a place for that, say in the bit about the children being in the right order … ?

Teacher:	He could maybe help to remind the children about when it is their turn. Thank you – that was very helpful. I need to think about the 'do' rather than the 'don't'.

Teachers are making adjustments all the time to accommodate difference and as one head teacher commented: 'It is about empowering us. Looking at what we have and thinking about different ways of using it. Some people might see this as plugging the gap; I see it as a pragmatic first response when there is a difficulty'.

42. How do coaches get better at coaching?

The real world is full of twists and turns. Coaching conversations will all have their own idiosyncrasies and some will work better than others. When we hit a sticking point then the reflective space coaches afford to others is also an important part of building their own practice. The following are a few ideas that budding coaches in schools have reported as being useful in building their confidence and competence in the coaching role.

Create a structure for mini-reflections. For example, after a coaching conversation, the coach could note down three things that went well. This could be related to what happened in the session or an aspect of their own coaching practice that they were pleased about. Some practitioners might also like to focus on one thing they might do differently next time and consider what difference they think it would make.

Find a coaching buddy to share experiences, ideas and frustrations with. In true coaching fashion, the coaching buddy can listen and ask questions:

- *Best hopes:* What are your best hopes from talking to me about this piece of work?

The answer to this will provide the context for the other questions. If the first answer is to get *some ideas* about the coaching they are doing, we would further enquire: 'Suppose we come up with some ideas that are useful to you, what are you hoping these ideas will lead to?'

- *Current successes:* Where have things got to in this piece of work (or whatever has been specified in their answer to the best hopes question)? What have you done that has been most useful?
- *Next signs:* What would tell you that the work was moving forward? What would the person you are working with say they are looking out for? What else will fuel your hope that change is possible in this situation?

Organise regular times for coaches to come together to share learning, look at specific issues or focus on elements of practice. When I was first learning about SF while working as an educational psychologist, an hour at the end of every alternate Friday afternoon was put aside with colleagues for SF reflections. One person would take the lead in each session around the aspect of practice they most wanted to concentrate on. An excellent exercise is to take a 'challenging answer' and think together of at least six different response questions.

Build a picture of the best version: A simple scale can be used where 10 denotes the coach you want to be. Coaches can help each other to celebrate current successes and calibrate future progress.

Consider the principles that underpin our questions, as these can help to reinforce the important 'soft aspects' of SF approach that drive what we ask and what we listen out for:

- Everyone is motivated towards something. Our job is to uncover what this is.
- However fixed a problem pattern is, there are always times when a person is doing some of the solution. The most economical approach is to help someone do more of what is working.
- Sometimes only the smallest changes are needed to set in motion a solution to a problem.
- Everyone has something they can do that will contribute to change and progress.

A senior teacher (ST) new into a coaching role was unsure how to go about supporting a struggling newly qualified teacher (NQT) who did not seem open to suggestions and ideas. The ST said she felt 'deskilled' and so she was asked to describe the capacities she usually drew on that were helpful in supporting others. The intention was to initially build a picture of what 'being supportive' looked like through the lens of past successes. The ST's useful qualities, already present but momentarily forgotten, could then be available to form a part of a future picture of success. Commenting that this was an unusual start, the ST talked about her calmness, approachability, her willingness to listen and her creativity borne out of a sound knowledge of the curriculum. We then looked at what had worked so far with the NQT. The ST had observed that feeding back something she had liked or inserting one of the teacher's ideas into a lesson she was teaching with her had seemed to aid discussions. The NQT also seemed a little more open if a discussion was framed as a 'quick chat' as opposed to a more formal meeting. From this basis, the conversation now turned to 'how to continue to build constructive dialogues' rather than 'how to work with this teacher'.

A couple of weeks later, the ST reported that things had gone much better than she had expected. Successful approaches had included finding out from the teacher what *she* wanted to work on, taking things slowly so that the teacher would not feel overwhelmed by what she was having to think about and planning together to co-create lessons. What had worked particularly well was asking the teacher what she (the ST) could do that would be most helpful.

Consultations with groups of staff

43. Using scales to support consultations over time

The first step when working with a group to staff is to establish a hoped-for difference that is relevant to all participants and broad enough to fully embrace the potential for change. Scales then offer a straightforward approach to bringing together a number of viewpoints around the criteria for success and highlighting what is already there to be built on. An advantage of a scale framework is that it can be continuously revisited to support a shared understanding of where things are in order to determine the next small steps.

A scale was used to structure a series of 15 minute discussions with four members of staff. They were all concerned about the level of disruption in 8D which often resulted in a disproportionate amount of time spent dealing with behaviour and a consequent reduction in the time spent on teaching.

Meeting 1

- The four staff members were asked to describe what a good lesson with 8D would look like. Time was spent bringing together their collective aspirations by asking them to consider what they would notice, what the students would notice and what others (head teacher, head of year, etc.) might comment on. It was important to elicit a rich description to provide many possibilities and benchmarks.
- A scale was introduced where the 10 was designated as a class full of good lessons and 0 the opposite. The teachers' current views of how things were going ranged from 2-8. Thus, it was possible to examine the small shoots of success that were already visible (some students wanting to learn, some settled lessons) followed up with questions about what was different at these times and the small actions that lay behind these successes.
- The staff were finally asked to continue to notice what was working with 8D and any small signs of progress.

Meeting 2

A couple of weeks later, although the situation with the class was by no means resolved, there were *some* things that had been better. Each member of staff was encouraged to outline anything that they had been pleased to notice and the group considered what they were learning that was useful with this class. 'Every success is a potential foundation for future progress: the stronger the foundation the greater the load it will bear' (Iveson et al. 2012: 117). Each improvement, however small, deserves examination of what was done, as this will give the best clues as to the behaviours and actions that are worth expanding. For example, the form tutor had changed the way she organised the hitherto dreaded morning registration period. There were often difficulties with students coming in late and a frustration with the time she had to spend settling small disputes. Taking the idea from the 'good lesson' discussion outlined above, she had begun by thinking about what a good registration period would look like. Key things she focused on were students being settled and occupied and her paying equal vigilance to those students who did settle and were co-operative or who needed her help. As a result, she decided to set little tasks and quizzes using copies of the Metro (free) newspaper for students to complete as they entered the classroom. Additionally, she adopted a basic behaviour system to note down and praise those students who came in and settled. The effects had been surprising. The students had risen to the challenge of the quizzes and as a consequence she was able to give more praise and have more conversations with individuals. However, it was the *impact* these changes had made which was fundamental to the 'load bearing' potential referred to above. The tutor felt that she had got to know her tutor group in a different way and the students themselves had started to relate differently through the debates which were occasionally sparked by a newspaper story.

Creating a momentum of things progressing makes it easier to look out for more signs of change in the right direction. So staff were again asked to each state two things they would be pleased to notice over the next couple of weeks and to carry on noticing those aspects of the classroom emerging which would support progress towards what they wanted.

Meeting 3

In the final meeting, the group returned to the original scale where the staff now described the class between the range of 6-8. All staff reported having different sorts of conversations with students. For example, a student receiving a detention from the English teacher had listened to and accepted the reasons; 'There is no way that would have happened before'. The form tutor had been pleased to notice that she was having more constructive dialogues with students who had previously avoided having their report cards signed at the end of the day. There was also agreement that the girls were 'more visible' and the class was now less tolerant of disruptions. These were significant differences which the staff felt could form the basis for more sustained developments.

It is easy amidst overwhelming difficulties to lose sight of our belief and our own self efficacy. Perhaps one of the most noticeable changes was the optimism and energy the teachers were now bringing into the room with 8D. One member of staff commented on how important the short meetings (15-20 minutes) had been in reminding her to keep looking at what was working. She had valued the support of knowing that there were others finding things difficult and that there was a shared approach amongst staff. There was an animated discussion about how to build on the strength of the girls in the class and introduce more group work. All the staff thought it would be useful to have half termly catch ups which could use a 'this is a great class' scale to keep track of how things were going.

44. Locating what is working and making it stronger

A group of teaching assistants (TAs) in a primary school were meeting together to find the best way to support a 7-year-old student called Vikresh in the classroom and in the playground. Many things had been tried with some occasional successes but with little longevity. It can be a temptation at this stage to offer more suggestions; however, much could be explored before going down this track.

Judging the pace and tone of a conversation is crucial with staff who have put a lot of time and effort into what they have been doing. Imagine that the meeting was like a game of 'rounders' with four bases. In order to reach the first base, it was important to acknowledge the toughness of the challenge the TAs were facing alongside the thought and creativity already evident in their work. 'It sounds like Vikresh has been the recipient of much care and thought as you have been trying to find a way through'. The TAs were then invited to consider: 'What has helped you all to walk that extra mile?' They talked about their own desire to make things work.

Moving towards the second base, the staff were now asked to consider what they *wanted*. Their best hopes were find a way to help Vikresh to play or work with other children without fighting, and a way of talking with him when difficulties occurred. The staff had previously indicated that there had been some small successes and it was now possible to pick out those successes that were most salient. Thus, for each small success in relation to talking, playing and working, the TAs were asked to elaborate on what they had done, the difference it made and their own ideas of why it might have worked. Statements such as: 'Well he was ok because he was playing football in the playground' or 'He was in a good mood that day' need to have the cover lifted off, to find what it was about playing football on *this* occasion that brought out the better side of Vikresh, as well as: 'What did you do that might have stoked his good mood for a little longer?' There are often many things to be discovered which, when nourished, have the potential to become a solution.

The third base highlighted future possibilities as the TAs explored what they would notice that would tell them that things were moving forwards. In describing what they would be noticing, the things they would be doing and how Vikresh would be responding, the TAs constructed a new narrative, based on their own expertise.

The final stretch to fourth base was about confidence and belief. Compiling a list of all the reasons for their current confidence in achieving the outcome they wanted was now bolstered by their knowledge of the situation, themselves and what worked. One TA commented: 'And as you can see, we do not give up easily'. A few weeks later, the TAs reported that things were much easier. In addition to the strategies they were trying out, they were also pleased about how well they were working as a team in continuing to share what was working and new ideas.

Meetings with parents and other professionals

45. Basic meeting structure

The question that is pertinent to all meetings is how to structure the discussion to ensure that people leave with enough to support their next steps. Michael Harker, an educational psychologist, has observed that in a 50 minute meeting as much as 40 minutes are taken up with information sharing about the nature and causes of difficulties leaving only 10 minutes for building solutions (Harker 2001: 33) and what is wanted is the flip side, where 40 minutes could be utilised to find workable solutions and ways forward that require minimal or no translation outside of a meeting. The SF framework has a number of elements outlined below that can support just such a change in emphasis so that more of the meeting is forward rather than backward looking.

Generic SF meeting structure

- Establishing the best hopes from the meeting. The outcome focus of looking at how things 'will be' rather than 'not be' can help support a shared view of a way forward.
- Using a scale where 10 represents the best hopes achieved, the meeting can explore what progress has been made in relation to the best hopes since the meeting was set

up (or reports were written), what has contributed to this progress and what signs of further progress the participants would be looking for.

- The final section of the meeting can be used to explore potential strategies to support gradual signs of progress.

46. Establishing the best hopes from the meeting

Having a clear idea of where you are heading at the beginning of a meeting helps to prevent the conversation drifting or going completely off track. 'How will you know that this meeting has been useful?' introduces a sense of purpose and a focus on the success criteria. Alternatively, a clarifying statement could be made: 'We are all here today to find a way forward for Jim ... Can we agree that we are here because we want Jim to be settled and learning in school?' (Harker 2001: 35). The first phrase encourages people to look at what can be done for Jim. This is not to negate the journey so far, but lengthy conversations about what has happened often lead to judgements about unhelpful actions or inaction. This, in turn, can lead to defensiveness and then much valuable time and energy gets diverted.

Where there are multiple participants it may be that initial responses require an additional question. If we assume that first answers are not an end in themselves but a *means* to an end, we can ask: 'And if (insert best hopes response) is achieved, what difference will it make?'

For example, a parent called to the school for a meeting might have the 'best hope' of not being summoned to meetings all the time to listen to complaints about his son:

And if you were not coming to school all the time for meetings what difference will it make?

Well things would certainly be better and calmer at home. After every meeting I try and talk to my son about his behaviour and we just get into an argument. There are so many arguments.

A student who has been asked to attend the meeting might want staff 'who are always on my back' to leave him alone.

And suppose you were left alone, what would be different?

I could just get on with things and not get wound up by the teachers.

At the same meeting the head of year's best hopes might include the student behaving in an acceptable manner and not flying off the handle when a teacher tries to discuss things with him.

And suppose he did behave in a more acceptable manner, what difference would that make?

Well, things would be more settled and we would be able to discuss things with him. Talk things through so we can sort them out.

On the surface, the individual best hopes might look very different. However, if we then explore what *difference* achievement of their best hopes would make there is greater possibility of finding a congruent way forward. In the above example, 'things being more settled and getting on with things', there is enough common ground to be able to move to a more detailed picture of what this would look like from each of their perspectives: 'Suppose tomorrow things were more settled, what would be the first sign? What other signs would tell you that things were different?'

47. Finding a starting point through parental aspirations

Being curious with parents about the aspirations they have for their children (and family) can also help in the negotiation and building of a collaborative venture.

- What are your best hopes for your child from being in school?
- What are you hoping for your child beyond school?
- Suppose things did change in a way that you hope for your child – what will be different now, and in the future?

Aspirational questions will not, on their own, sort everything out. However, the more we ask about and clarify what is being sought, the easier it is to find a starting point. For example, a parent wants her child to get a good job in the future as a route to being independent and self-sufficient. Independence and self-sufficiency can reside in a job and also in many steps along the way towards this. This could be further explored with questions such as:

- What might you be noticing about her in the mornings/when she gets back from school that would fit with her getting on as you would like her to be?
- What will tell you that James is starting to make progress towards this (insert aspiration)?
- What will your daughter say you and the school do that is most helpful to them in keeping on track?
- Imagine your son 10 or 15 years into the future, being interviewed about how they got to where they are. What might he be saying about what his parents and the school had done, when he was younger, that best supported his current achievements?

The strong views of Mrs Leyton

There are many reasons why parents may appear unhappy with what is happening in school and there may be times when they are justified. How they present themselves is a different matter, and if the parent is being abusive, or racist or sexist, or threatening, this needs to be dealt with by management in line with school policy. Outside of this, the key SF principles that will govern a conversation with an unhappy parent include finding a commonality, validation and possibility.

Mrs Leyton's son Raul was finding it difficult to settle to his work, was struggling in his friendships and could often be observed on the periphery of activities. Mrs Leyton had a history of coming into the school and shouting at staff and children. Most recently, Mrs Leyton had been very angry about another child in the school who had upset Raul, and had berated the child in the playground at the end of the day. Repeated requests from staff to talk with them to help sort the situation out were ignored and in the end Mrs Leyton had been banned from the school premises. Undeterred, she would stand outside the school fence and harangue the child from the pavement. It took several repeated requests from Mr Brown, the head teacher, until finally Mrs Leyton agreed to come to a meeting.

On the morning of the meeting, Mrs Leyton made it very clear that she only had 20 minutes to spare, and that she was fed up with the number of times she was called by the school for 'trivial matters'.

Mr Brown started by asking Mrs Leyton 'What would you like for Raul in school?', giving his reason that it was important to hear from her about how *she* would like things to be for him. Mrs Leyton began to talk about Raul doing well in his learning and having friends. This involved a little detour into how difficult some of the other children were and the unfairness of how things were dealt with.

When we are listening to a number of comments or details we have a choice about what to expand on and what we let go. In SF practice, what governs this choice is focusing on those aspects of the conversation which are most likely to support the outcome that is wanted. Many of Mrs Leyton's comments were about what she did not like or was unhappy with. So Mr Brown persisted in drawing out details of what Mrs Leyton *did* want for Raul and what difference this would make. In this way, he was able to validate her ideas and to acknowledge that they, as a school, would want the same things. He also talked about what the school liked about Raul and asked Mrs Leyton what she thought her son was good at. There was further discussion about the ups and downs of children's development and Mrs Leyton agreed that things did not always go smoothly. She talked about her worries regarding Raul's learning and Mr Brown agreed to explore this further with the class teacher.

Within the context of 'ups and downs', Mr Brown began to ask Mrs Leyton about the best ways to deal with things when they were not going so well, and in particular how they could let each other know. At this point, Mrs Leyton pointed a finger at Mr Brown and said: 'Now I can see what you are doing'. However, she continued to talk about how she was not happy when Raul came home upset about things that had happened which seemed unfair. During this, Mr Brown listened and acknowledged so that Mrs Leyton felt heard, although not necessarily entirely agreed with. Raul, who had been waiting outside the room, was invited to join the meeting at this point. He entered somewhat hesitantly, as he had often witnessed his mother shouting at staff. Mrs Leyton, Raul and Mr Brown proceeded to negotiate a clear system that would work when difficulties occurred. At the end of the meeting Mrs Leyton turned to Raul and said: 'And I don't want to hear that you have been rude to Mr Brown here'.

The meeting ended with a handshake and, for the first time, a 'thank you' from Mrs Leyton. For several years after Raul had left the school, Mr Brown would often bump into him and his mother in the local area. He was always given a smile and a mini-update about how Raul was getting on at secondary school.

(Martin Brown head teacher, personal communication)

48. What if the student is not at the meeting?

If the student is not at the meeting, it is still possible for those present to outline their own views of what the student might say. Briefly considering the world through the eyes of a student can sometimes widen perspectives, possibilities and routes to solutions.

An inclusion manager (IM) was unsure about the best way to support a Year 9 student called Sarah who was very unsettled and having a lot of arguments. She had tried lots of things but did not really know what was helping. In the following extract, as more ideas came to mind, so the inclusion manager began to attach more significance to the small everyday things that were important underpinnings for any future work with Sarah.

Coach:	So you have tried many things. Some things work and some don't. If Sarah were at this meeting, what do you think *she* would she say that she has most valued about the way you have worked with her?
IM:	Gosh. I don't know. Probably nothing.
Coach:	So maybe nothing. If she did say something, what is it that you think she would be mentioning?
IM:	Well. I always say hello to her and smile and sometimes she smiles back.
Coach:	Ok. Smiling. What else?
IM:	Well if I hear about anything that has gone well from another teacher then I always try and pass it on to her.
Coach:	And you think she likes that?
IM:	Yes. Because she hears lots of things people don't like. And I guess it sort of balances that out a bit.
Coach:	And when things have been tough for Sarah. What, at those times, do you think she would say she appreciates?
IM:	Definitely giving her time to calm down before I try and talk with her.
Coach:	Ok. What else?
IM:	Letting her start with whatever she wants to say. Definitely not saying 'we need to talk about this'!
Coach:	Anything else?
IM:	Hmm. Oh yes. Sometimes if there is a younger student working in the unit she might help them with something and that seems to calm her. And I can thank her for her help which she seems to like.
Coach:	And what do you think she might say she most appreciates about the way that you talk with her - whatever you are saying?
IM:	Just that I am always pleased to see her. Whatever the circumstances.

A mother had been asked to attend a meeting with the school counsellor with her daughter Princess. However, Princess had been delayed at a sporting event. While they were waiting, the mother started to talk to the counsellor about Princess's difficult behaviour at home. A major source of tension was the fact that Princess never said 'thank you' and this lack of appreciation was causing arguments. In the following extract, asking the mother to consider what 'appreciation' would look like through the eyes of Princess helped to move the discussion away from the dichotomy of 'does or doesn't show appreciation' towards a wider landscape where appreciation could appear in many forms.

Counsellor:	So can I ask you an odd question?
Mother:	Yes.
Counsellor:	If Princess was in the room, how would she say she shows her appreciation for the things that you do?
Mother:	Gosh. I have no idea.
Counsellor:	Have a guess. You know your daughter well. How would she say she shows her appreciation when you do something?
Mother:	*(Pause)* Well she would probably say that she nods her head.
Counsellor:	And would Princess describe this nod as her equivalent to the words 'thank you?'
Mother:	*(laughs)* You know I think she would.
Counsellor:	What else might Princess say she does?

49. Clarifying priorities: multiple scaling

It can feel very overwhelming when there are a lot of things to work on and difficult to know where to start. 'Multi-scales' (Iveson et al. 2012: 95) offer a structure which can not only capture the complexity of situations but also determine what to pay attention to in the first instance. Rather than try and subsume multiple issues in one scale, each issue is given its own scale.

Take, for example, a situation where there are four major concerns. Imagine a large piece of paper where there are four vertical scales with 10 at the top and 0 at the bottom. The 0 can be broadly informed by the stated issue (what is not wanted, for example, refusing to do work or hitting other children) and the 10 could be negotiated as the successful resolution (what is wanted, for example, confidence in learning or friendships with children). The importance of clarifying the 10 is fundamental to SFP, establishing a sense of direction on which to build the conversation.

The session can then follow a classic scale conversation, the only difference being that the questions are repeated several times to accommodate the different scales. So, once the current numbers of where things are at have been established, several things that could represent small successes already visible can be recorded for each scale. If appropriate, the question can be framed as: 'What has stopped things from being any lower?' in preference to: 'How come things are that high?' as the latter can communicate a lack of understanding of the seriousness of the situation. The result would be a collective list, over the four scales, of all the positive elements currently residing in the situation and visually represented as a platform across the lower half of the paper. The intention is not to persuade the staff that things are actually better than they think, rather to highlight those aspects of what is happening which could support the changes they were wanting.

Two or three very small signs of progress for each scale can produce a list of up to 12 realistic possibilities for the future spread across the four scales. These might be big things or little things. As they are brought into view, so potential pathways towards them are also opened up. Change in one area can also have a knock-on effect. For example, 'Suppose things moved one point up on the "Having good friendships with other children" scale, what difference will this make to the "Confidence in learning" scale?' In this way, scales can be interwoven.

A group of staff who were concerned about an 8-year-old boy called Pedro used multiple scaling to help consider the aspects of his behaviour and learning that were causing concern: his relationship with staff, working collaboratively with other children and building his resilience when he made a mistake. Using 3 scales gave staff a clearer focus. They paid particular attention to 'building a good relationship with staff' in the first instance and monitored the difference this made to the other scales. They commented that breaking down what had seemed like an impossible task into the individual scales had helped them to refine their focus and energy. It had been uplifting to realise the many things that *were* working and also to pay attention to the small changes that happened over time.

50. When things are tough

When things are not going well or are seemingly hopeless, there is danger of skidding into solution *forced* practice where we either try to persuade someone that things are not as bad as they say or we jump in too soon with suggestions. At these times, SF practitioners will keep by their side assumptions that can rekindle hope and provide platforms from which people can begin to find their own way forward.

Assumption of possibilities

Even in the toughest of situations there is often something constructive to be found. The best questions sit easily with the current situation and at the same time hold the possibility of change. We want to encourage the biggest step into the solution world that a person can manage.

- When have things been closest to how you would like them to be? What would be your ideas about what was happening at this time that was different?
- If there is a chance of moving forward, even though it looks unlikely at the moment, I wonder what the basis for that possibility is?
- How confident are you, on a 0-10 scale, that things can get back on track? What contributes to that confidence?
- Even though it is like looking for a needle in a haystack, what has she potentially got going for her that we could work with?

Assumption of competence: the parent you want to be

There may be times when a member of staff would want to question a parent's behaviour towards their child, and it is a delicate matter as to how to talk to someone about this. If there is a clear child protection issue, then it would need to be taken up by the appropriate responsible manager in accordance with school protocol. However, it also raises the broader question about how we can work with parents to effect change in a way that does not alienate them or further convince them that theirs are the best or only courses of action. Taking a critical position often sets a precedent for the other person to harden their own view. Polarity in discussions rarely leads to any lasting transformations and so to try and persuade or tell a parent can have the opposite to the desired effect.

The use of questions which have within them an assumption of competence can be useful in addressing an issue in a respectful and non-judgemental manner. They afford the space for parents to enter into a dialogue rather than feeling the need to defend their position. For example, the practitioner was asked to have a discussion with a group of parents at a children's centre 'stay and play' session where staff were feeling that the parents were not allowing their pre-school children the space to play, explore and make mistakes. Rather than challenge this, the following questions were used to create an open context within which to think with the parents about the best help to give their children.

- How do you know when to step in and when to step out?
- How do you know what is the best sort of support to give to your child in this situation?
- How do you know when your child is ready to take over again?

Although these questions were not easy to answer, for some it opened up the opportunity to discuss worries about their children crying and how this prompted them to step in and sort things out. Using a combination of observation regarding the skills and strategies their children were using and discussion about the skills the parents would like to see them developing, the parents began to build their own approaches to supporting their children. This provided them with a rich source of ideas when it came to looking ahead to the children starting school. By helping to build their child's own portfolio of skills, parents can help them to navigate their way through the ever-changing circumstances in school and beyond.

Assumption of good will

There may be times when there is a need to talk with parents more directly about issues such as attendance. These are not easy situations to deal with but a good starting point is to assume 'good will' on the part of the parent, that they do want their child to have a good life, in fact a better life than they have had themselves. 'If' questions can be very helpful here. 'I know you have doubts about how useful school can be for your child, but *if* it worked out well for them, how would you know?' Additional questions can be used as appropriate: 'Who in your family – grandparents, aunts, whoever – have hopes that education will be of benefit? What would they hope to see *if* it were to be beneficial?'

In the final event it may be necessary to state clearly to the parent the fact – which they will probably know only too well – that it is a legal requirement for them to ensure their child is in education and the school might be forced to initiate a statutory system with increasingly severe consequences for the parents (and child). 'I assume that you don't want this to happen, and I'd very much like to find a way we can work together to avoid us having to go down the legal route ... '

Assumption of hope: *the power of words*

Parents need to feel hopeful about their child and we, as practitioners, need to do the child justice in the way we represent them. Whilst I (YA) was working as an educational psychologist in a London borough, a parent requested a tribunal hearing for her son, David, who had recently started in Year 7 at a secondary school. Although David had been allocated additional support, his mother wanted a specialist boarding school for students with dyslexia. I was asked to complete an assessment and report on behalf of the local authority. The mother also paid for a private psychologist's report. The tribunal ruling was in favour of the local authority and upheld David's placement in a mainstream school. Straight after this judgement, David's mother came running after me down the corridor. As I braced myself for her understandable disappointment, imagine my surprise when she thanked me. She talked about her despair at reading the private psychologist's report which had left her feeling as though her son could not, and would never be able to, achieve anything. In contrast, reading my description of her son which looked at his skills and at the things that were important to him, gave her hope about him in the present and in the future.

Assumption of hope: *the position of the worker*

Sometimes we are faced with a situation which is so complex that we as workers struggle to think about a way forward. However, if we also move into the same place of hopelessness as the people we are working with, it is harder to search for, or see, the potential clues for difference or change. An inclusion manager asked to discuss a family where there were so many issues – housing, finances, children struggling in school, difficult relationships at home – that she could not see a way through. While it is important to empathise, as workers we also need to find a way to maintain our own hope and belief that difference is possible. The practitioner asked the inclusion manager: 'Suppose you were to enter the next conversation with this family with the belief that, despite the weight of concerns, change or difference is in some way possible, how would you communicate this without directly raising it?' After some thought she replied: 'I will take some energy into the room'. She was asked to say more about how this would show and what the family would notice about her. Two weeks later, the inclusion manager talked about a recent meeting with the family. Although the situation was still tough, she felt that the way she looked at it had changed. Rather than feeling hopeless, she had been able to step back and think creatively with the family about the small opportunities available to them, particularly around the support for the children in school and support for the mother in handling things with them at home. Under the umbrella of 'being at your best' the inclusion manager had also boosted the mother's confidence in seeking out additional help from other agencies.

51. Pupil progress meetings and beyond

Promoting change by focusing on change

A few weeks before the pupil progress review meeting, a class of Year 5 students were given a slot at the end of a day to think about their learning journey throughout the year. Using a series of scales to obtain a thumbnail sketch across a range of areas looking at their learning and behaviour, the students were asked to focus on what they had been doing that they were pleased to notice (current successes), anything that they would particularly like to focus on, change or do differently (future possibilities) and two things they had learnt about themselves that would be good for their learning in their Year 6 SATs year (skills and resources).

Parents were also asked to think, in advance, about two things they had been pleased to notice at home about their child's learning and something they would like to see more of. Although not all parents came to the pupil progress meetings having engaged in this activity, the forward thinking of the teacher and the students provided an initial focus that could be built upon. By amplifying what was already happening, the conversation was about *assisting* rather than *starting* a change process. The descriptive focus on 'signs of progress to be noticed' rather than 'actions to be done' encouraged the students and parents to carry on generating ideas after the discussion rather than just sticking to the stated suggestions.

The learning journey scales for the Year 5 pupil review meeting continued to be used afterwards. Time was set aside each week for students to reflect on how their learning had gone, the good things they had done and their 'tomorrow ideas'. Feedback from the parents indicated that the 'scale snapshots' gave them a much better understanding of what was happening in school and they enjoyed the more positive feedback from their children about how things were going.

Meetings around organisational developments

52. Linking visions, policies and practice

All schools have a 'vision and ethos' statement and a wide range of policies. Although the 'vision' or policy conducts, it is the orchestra and players that make the music. Every idea identified in the vision or in a policy is only as useful as its relevance to the day-to-day life in school.

The senior leadership team in a start-up secondary school, Year 7 only in the first year, wanted to formulate a behaviour policy that was firmly rooted in practice and drew on the expertise and experience of the staff. Thus, rather than work downwards from the policy, the school decided to work outwards from the visible hoped-for differences that an effective policy would make to school life. Locating this successful future provided a context where the policy was seen as more than a set of actions: it represented a set of values that would govern what was done and how it was done.

Activity 1: the successful future

Staff in groups were asked to 'Imagine it has been a year of success in creating a strong and constructive ethos in the school to support the promotion of positive behaviour' and to consider the future 'evidence' from a 360 degree viewpoint of staff, students, parents and other key stakeholders. Describing what others will notice brings a richness to the detail.

These broad brush-stroke details were then evaluated. Staff were asked to highlight those things that, at the end of a successful year, would have had the greatest impact on building an ethos to support policy and practice. For each detail deemed to have a big impact further examination, still from the position of future success, looked at how it would have been initiated and maintained, and the difference it would have made. For example, establishing a clear expectation for behaviour. This would initially have been introduced in the first week through assemblies and class-based discussions where the rules and reasons would have been explained and students would have had the opportunity to ask questions. These expectations would be reinforced by a consistency across all staff. What this would look like was also delineated.

Activity 2: what works

The foundations for success in schools reside in the classroom and in the relationships that are built with, and between, students and staff. The second activity, therefore, explored how the staff went about building trusting and productive relationships with students, and their approaches to dealing with challenges. Staff were asked to consider:

- At its best, what do the first 10 minutes with a class look like in promoting positive behaviour?
- At your best, how do you communicate your expectations and how would your class know that you enjoyed teaching them?
- What are your ways of dealing with an incident that offer the best ways forward?
- What are the best ways you have found of following up an incident?

Activity 3: team cohesion

Staff wellbeing and staff support are an essential ingredient in any successful approach to behaviour, particularly when mindful of the considerable challenges that behaviour can pose. Thus, the staff group were invited to outline the details, and value, of a team working well together:

- If I was to spend a day with your team at its best, what would you be pleased for me to be picking up on? What would tell me, and the students, about the high level of cohesion and support between staff members?
- What would parents and visitors to the school notice in particular?

- What difference would this cohesion make to the establishment and maintenance of a strong and constructive ethos around behaviour in the school?

A discussion evolved from this about how staff could support each other and also the types of conversations that would take place should something need to be addressed.

Activity 4: from practice to principles

Finally, from all of the discussions, the staff were asked to draw out some of the guiding principles which underpinned their ideas about the effective setting up and development of behavioural systems and routines in a school. These formed the basis of the behaviour policy.

Reviewing

Three months into the first term, a twilight staff meeting was held to review progress. Broad scales (10 = the best, 0 = the worst) were used to obtain a thumbnail sketch around each of the nine priority areas outlined in the behaviour policy; for example, 'To encourage self-discipline and a reflective mind-set where pupils are able to recognise and manage their own behaviour'. These scales offered a prime opportunity for staff to look at and admire how far they had come and all that had contributed to this. In small groups, staff noted all the achievements for their numbers on each scale, and what had been most influential in bringing these about. Several scales were cross-referenced. For example, 'What difference has the successes in encouraging the reflective mindset of pupils made to student responsibility or parental confidence?' At the end of the staff meeting there was a clear indication of what was working well (leading by example and building positive relationships) and what needed more attention (forming positive partnerships with parents). With this clarity of focus it was easy to consider small signs of progress in these areas, whilst for the large majority of the nine indicators the clear message was to carry on doing what was already working.

A year later, the head teacher had welcomed his second cohort of Year 7 students to the school, greatly aided by the new Year 8 who embodied and modelled expectations. Looking back, he felt that the initial staff meeting had set up the core values which governed all that had happened. By incorporating staff beliefs, he felt the session had done more than just take the staff along, as it was these beliefs that guided expectations about what would happen and the methods for bringing these about. The encouragement of an open and practical dialogue with staff ideally feeds upwards into policies and downwards into the life of schools in a way that creates a sense of joint ownership. The head teacher felt this approach encouraged staff interest, commitment and a stake in making it work. The detail of the initial discussion and the use of scales had made subsequent review discussions efficient and effective. They had helped the staff to feel an achievement when specific aspects of what they were hoping to achieve were observed in action. (Richard Paul head teacher)

53. Locating and building on strengths

Strengthening what works

It is often the case that all the necessary ingredients for success are already in place. Examining what is already happening through a SF lens can help to pick out the relevant aspects to amplify. This relevance is determined by the outcome that is wanted. Amplification helps take these 'instances of success' further towards solutions.

A group of staff at an offsite unit for secondary-aged students wanted to improve their working relationships with parents. The parents and students often arrived with a history of difficult experiences with, and within, schools. The staff wanted them to have a different experience. The starting point with this staff group was to explore: 'What do we already do that works well with engaging parents?' Asking: 'What difference do these actions make?' helps to locate those ideas that have the biggest impact in line with what the practitioners and the school are trying to achieve.

What emerged was the value of paying attention to the first contacts with parents when their child joined the school, although staff felt the ideas were equally valuable as part of building an ongoing relationship with parents. Several ideas were then considered. For example, inviting parents to talk about the 'good things that are happening at home' or if things were a bit rocky, something small they had managed to keep going. This would provide the opportunity for the staff to listen with a 'constructive ear' (Lipchick 1986) for parental qualities. A successful team needs all its players, so a recognition of parental skills would be an important underpinning for future possibilities. Having an oasis of good news would also mean that the contact between parents and school did not focus only on difficulties.

The staff also felt that exploring with parents what 'good working together' would look like right from the beginning would help make both parental and school expectations explicit. Finding out from parents what has worked previously in school or with their child, even if things might have been difficult, would also provide clues of what would be helpful.

Reinforcing strengths

Change happens more effectively and robustly when it rests on strengths. If an organisation doesn't pay attention to its talents, then it is easy for them to slip out of sight. 'People bring with them solution patterns as well as problem patterns and change is based on doing more of what people are already doing' (Ratner et al. 2012: 30).

> An interim head teacher was asked to support a school following an inspection which had highlighted many difficulties and areas in need of improvement. The current head teacher had left without notice and the staff were understandably demoralised. The head teacher's opening gambit in the first staff meeting was to start with a 'good things list': groups of staff were asked to record at least 20 things that the school did well from their point of view and the successful strategies which underpinned these. These lists were then displayed in the staffroom as a testament to all that was good in the school and the local authority inspector

visiting the school in the following weeks commented on the increased energy and morale among the staff. However, this was more than just a 'feel good' exercise – although in itself staff morale is an essential ingredient in any change process. The lists provided a foundation on which to address the improvements the inspectorate was looking for. The strengths identified were also deployed to help settle and support Year 6 in preparation for their SATs at the end of the year. Even though it was a period of continued difficulties, the school received a letter from the government commending it for being in the top 100 most improved schools in the country in relation to its SAT results. The incoming substantive head teacher felt the underpinnings of strengths, resources and staff morale were an important feature in his subsequent guidance of the school out of special measures and into the world of 'competence'.

(Martin Brown, head teacher)

Increasing opportunities for appreciation and feedback

A culture of mutual appreciation is about shifting patterns of attention. How we talk about what we see and what we do shapes an ethos that supports change, difference and challenge. Following attendance at a SF training, a head teacher decided to change the material displayed on the year notice boards in the staffroom. Data about students causing concern (students on report, attending the external exclusion room and those who had been excluded) was collated in folders. This left space on the boards for details about the successes in the school (those students who had been successfully reintegrated back into class, students who had made great progress academically, the stars of track and stage and so on) to greet staff as they entered the staff room.

How teams do justice to their strengths and how good teams support each other is especially pertinent during tough times. Public celebrations of success, by definition, can highlight staff contributions. In busy environments, it can be expedient to formalise these opportunities for appreciation. For example, setting aside a few minutes at the beginning of a staff meeting for staff to share a 'sparkling moment' (White 1998: 202), something that has gone well, or share constructive things staff have noticed about others. As one primary school teacher commented: 'It is easy to become buried under the day-to-day pressures in school. Knowing the staff meeting was coming up made me stick my head above the parapet for a moment. Once you start looking there is lots to see'.

'Creating a discipline of appreciation for specific contributions to the team's work will add to the team's confidence, level of performance and expectation of success, factors clearly associated with job satisfaction and retention of staff' (Ratner et al. 2012: 215).

References

Harker, M. (2001) How to Build Solutions at Meetings. In Y. Ajmal and I. Rees (Eds.) *Solutions in Schools*. London: BT Press.

Iveson, C., George, E. and Ratner, H. (2012) *Brief Coaching: A Solution Focused Approach*. London: Routledge.

Lipchick, E. (1986) The Purposeful Interview. *Journal of Strategic and Systemic Therapies* 5 (1/2): 88–99.

O'Hanlon, B. and Beadle, S. (1996) *A Field Guide to PossibilityLand: Possibility Therapy Methods*. London: BT Press.

Ratner, H., George, E., and Iveson, C. (2012) *Solution Focused Brief Therapy: 100 Key Points and Techniques*. London: Routledge.

White, M. (1998) *Re-authoring Lives: Interviews and Essays*. Adelaide, South Australia: Dulwich Centre Publications.

Part 5   Working with groups around specific issues

54. Introduction: structure of sessions

When there a number of people with a similar issue, one approach can be to bring them together as a group (for examples of SF group work, see Metcalf 1998; Ratner and Yusuf 2015; Sharry 2007; Young 2009). Apart from the obvious benefit of time in working with several participants at once, group members can learn a lot from each other and the 'don't know' responses can be filled out with contributions from others. Change happens when we invite people into different ways of 'viewing' or 'doing' and the interactions between group members can also intensify solutions and useful ways forward.

Structure of a 1st session

The aim of the first session is to establish the group context and the purposefulness of the work. The following sequence encourages a gradual building of ideas within a clear structure. However, a challenge of group work is how to keep everyone involved and maintain the momentum, so that individuals leave with more than they started with. As will be illustrated later in the chapter, the relative emphasis on each part of the process will vary.

- Introductions and starting the search for resources: 'Something you have been pleased to notice in the last week'.
- Setting ground rules: 'How will we know we're working well together?'
- Establishing the purpose of the group and the individual 'best hopes' within this: 'How will you know coming to this group has been useful to you?' or, where the preferred outcome has been agreed upon in advance, more specifically: 'How will you know that this group has been helpful to you in "getting better at working with other students?" or "supporting your child during their exams?"'
- Building preferred future descriptions of when these best hopes have been achieved: 'What will you be noticing tomorrow?' or 'How will you know you are at your best?' Time frames such as: 'What will you be noticing different by the end of term?' might also be used.
- Using scale questions to examine current progress and all that has contributed to this.

- Asking participants to discuss how they will know they have moved forward 1 point.
- Endings: acknowledgement of difficulties, highlighting of qualities and capacities that could be the basis of progress, recapping of actions that have already been taken towards what is wanted and signs of hope.

2nd and subsequent sessions

The aim of the 'follow up sessions' is literally to follow up on any signs of progress made since the last meeting. The list of questions could include:

- What's better? What progress has each of you made?
- (If things have not improved for someone) How have you coped? What have you done to stop things from getting worse?
- Scale questions to 'quantify' the progress.
- Looking at further signs of progress (1 point forward).
- Compliments (highlighting qualities, as before).

Whether in first or subsequent sessions, the same supplementary questions are used to build more detailed descriptions, such as:

- What else?
- How did that show? What was a sign of that happening?
- Who has noticed? What have they noticed?
- What has been the effect on others?
- What effect (on others) has that had on you?

Group work with students

The generic SF framework can be adapted to work with groups set up to address a wide range of issues. For example, students identified as having a particular issue with anger or friendships, a peer group meeting to discuss how to manage bullying (Young 2009), students needing support with their confidence or organisation. Later in the chapter, we will describe work where the focus was on mediation between groups of students.

55. Mobilising resources and useful qualities

Students describing their own resources

Starting sessions with questions that help students to remember the good things that they can do is not simply a 'feel good' exercise. The business of change requires a currency of competency and we need to help students to discover or remember ways of thinking and behaving that might be useful for them. Examples of questions might include:

- Something you have been pleased to notice (pointing attention to what is working).
- Something you are good at (everyone has something they can do).
- Your proudest moment (reconnecting students with their pride in themselves).
- A challenge you have faced and come through (highlighting the student's capacities to make changes).

Inspiring students to believe in themselves and the possibility that they can move forward will assist in the move away from a complaint-saturated story, as is shown in this extract from work with a group of Year 5 students.

Practitioner:	How come the school thought you would be good people to have in a group?
Student A:	We are bad students ... always in trouble.
Practitioner:	Are you the only students who get into trouble in Year 5?
Student B:	No.
Practitioner:	So, what did the school see in you that made them think you might have something to offer in a group situation?
Student B:	*(After a few 'don't knows' from others)* We've got some good ideas.
Student C:	We're good at sorting things out.
Student A:	And we're enthusiastic ... and energetic!

Helping useful qualities to emerge can help to establish 'the group that anyone would want to work with'!

Students hearing about their resources

Although it is desirable for students to provide their own eulogies, it can sometimes help if we oil the wheels. A learning mentor told a group of Year 7 boys who had been in a lot of trouble that she had sent a round robin to staff asking for comments about the *good* things the students brought to their learning and the classes they attended. There was silence as the boys listened with obvious delight to what had been said and surprise that some teachers saw them in this way. The learning mentor later heard from an English teacher, who had sent a comment about one of the students, that following this session there was a noticeable difference in the way he behaved in her class.

Using activities to help students discover their resources

Using ice-breaker activities at the beginning of a group (although they are equally useful if inserted at any time) can also provide a 'stage' on which the 'actors' can demonstrate and examine their capacities and strategies in situ. These have been used successfully with students up to KS3, however, their use will depend on the maturity of the group.

- The students can be divided into groups and set the task of completing a short activity. Examples might include lining up according to a variety of criteria such as hair length or completing a problem-solving task such as building a tower out of their trainers. At the end of the task the students can be asked to discuss what they and others in their group did that enabled the task to be successfully completed. This helps to uncover their useful behaviours and strategies around team work, building solutions and so on. Adding an additional instruction to complete the task without talking, encourages students to pay attention to themselves and each other in a different way.

- A focused observation could be tailored to specific aspects of desired behaviour. For example, a Year 6 group, brought together to build their collaborative working skills, were divided into two. One half completed a problem-solving task (using an array of materials to build a specified structure), the other half observed and recorded what worked well in terms of 'listening to each other' and 'helping each other'. These were fed back before the two groups swapped around.

When strengths are based on the reality of small aspects of behaviours already present, they are readily available to be further shaped and used again. It is not uncommon for actions discussed at the beginning of groups to begin to make an appearance at other times. Thus, from observing and describing, the route to doing and ownership is laid.

56. Establishing 'ground rules' for the group

Involving students in establishing the ground rules accentuates that their views are being sought. Any additional ground rules not raised by the students can be introduced by the adults and issues of confidentiality may need to be directly addressed in line with the school's policy.

Opening questions: 'What will tell us that this group is at its best?' or 'What are 10 things that will be signs of this group working well together?'
Questions regarding more specific ground rules: 'How can we ensure that the things we talk about are kept in the group?' or 'What would be the best way to think about lateness, loo breaks and the like?'
Hypothetical questions to consider ground rules: 'Obviously if someone is ill and misses a meeting that's not their fault, but what if they miss two meetings? Should they still be allowed to return to the group?'

57. Supporting forward-looking conversations

Group names

The 'looking ahead' focus in SFP can be reflected in the group name. For example, the students in an 'anger management' group renamed themselves 'Project for Change' (Ratner and Yusuf 2015). 'Anger management' is related to the problem, 'project for change' is related to a shift towards something different. Even the self-named 'Dark Warriors' from Year 7 were interested in being the best they could be and, for them, the name was aspirational, if a little unconventional.

Finding out what students want from the group

Although the purpose of the group has often been defined by the school, it is still possible to guide conversations towards more individual hopes and achievements. For example, although the whole group might be asked the same broad future focused question such as: 'Suppose tomorrow you are at your best in (stated purpose of the group), what will you and others notice?' or 'What do you hope to achieve by Progress Review Day?' (Ratner and Yusuf op cit.), the specific details from each student will be different. Rounds of questions work well in giving everyone a say with the added value of hearing the contributions of other group members:

- 'I'm going to go around three times and each time I would like to hear things you will be pleased to notice yourself doing tomorrow that will be signs of progress.'
- Variations can be inserted at any time – for example, at the beginning of the third round, students can be asked what they think their friends, teachers or parents will notice different about them tomorrow.

If a student has misunderstood the question or given an answer that is too vague, they can be asked a couple of supplementary questions, for example, 'What will you be *doing* differently when you are calmer?' At any time, if a student appears unable to answer, they can have a 'pass' for that round; in our experience, a student who 'passes' will usually have something to say after everyone else has had their turn.

Sometimes, a common theme emerges from the 'rounds'. For example, a group of students talking about getting better grades might all mention 'saying no' to friends as something they would notice. 'Saying no to friends' can be further explored by looking at the difference this would make, what is already working and signs of progress. This can then be interwoven with 'getting better grades'. For example, 'Suppose you did find a way of "saying no to friends", what difference will that make to your grades?' Or conversely, 'What difference will "getting better grades" make to how you respond to your friends?' This two-way interaction exponentially increases the routes into change. The relative importance assigned by each individual student to the different parts will determine what they pay most attention to.

58. Using a scale

Scales provide a ready-made structure that can support individual views within a group context. Take, for example, a group with the aim of 'increasing confidence in taking exams' or 'improving behaviour'. The description of the 10, total confidence or behaviour at its best, might be broadly similar. However, the numbers given by individual students and the accompanying descriptions provide the space for a wide difference of focus and actions.

Where are things at the moment?

Numbers provide an opening for achievements to emerge. Sometimes we can lever this opening a little wider. A group of Year 8 boys, all a hair's breadth from exclusion, agreed that they did want to stay in the school. On a scale where 10 denoted 'things are going well in school' they placed themselves between 0-2. Given this, and the fact that they had all been in a lot of trouble, the group were asked if they had ever been any *lower* on the scale. The boys immediately extended the scale to minus 25! Seen within *this* context, the 0-2 ratings heralded quite a significant success and turned the tone of the conversation towards efficacy and competency. The students were keen to outline all the things they had been doing to get themselves out of the minuses, including avoiding fights by not going around in large groups, getting some good grades and making themselves invisible around staff who they felt had a very negative view of them.

If the 0-2 numbers had represented their lowest point, the students could have been asked what they had done to stop things from being even lower or how come they were managing to still remain in the school. The principle is the same, providing the opportunity to look at what is working in a situation so that any developments start from a solid base.

Small signs of progress

Students themselves are often the best judge of the pace and progress that is right for them, so it can be useful to check if the group are satisfied with where things are or if they would like to be any higher. Not only did the boys want to be higher but, inspired by the minus 25, the scale was extended, literally with hastily added bits of flip chart paper, to a 100. The 100 represented an aspiration and was followed up with exploring signs of progress towards this. For each sign of things moving forwards, there was the opportunity for further questioning to help students value the significance of the little things:

- What would be the smallest sign of that happening (for example, 'keeping my cool') tomorrow?
- What would be the smallest step towards that (for example, 'not getting into silly games that lead to fights')?
- What would give your teachers a clue in the next week that *that* was growing (for example, 'focusing on my work in class')?

Had the boys *not* been interested in things progressing higher, one option would have been to go back to their earlier statement about wanting to stay in the school. The focus would have been on how adept they were at judging how good things were and, if they noticed things slipping further down, what they had learned that would be helpful.

The perspective of others

The Year 8 students had mentioned the negative views of some teachers. It is always useful to bring in the perspectives of others, particularly in the school context where there will usually be a number of adults taking an interest in how things are going. The students were asked to consider:

- 'Where would the school or significant members of staff need to see you on the scale in order to take their foot off the pedal? What will they be picking up on?' These details need to be recognised and brought into the frame.
- 'Who would be the "first", "middle" or "last" person to notice that you are making changes?' This also takes into account the variability in response that students will experience.

Time was then spent looking at the students' ways of dealing with this varied response – in line with their desire to stay in the school. Keeping all parts of the conversation connected to the preferred outcome ensures that both questions and answers do not go adrift from the purpose of the work. Amongst other things, the boys talked about the value of building a strong relationship with some teachers.

   The group continued to attend for six sessions during which the small incremental steps they were taking became more visible to the school and effective for them. None of the boys were excluded.

59. Questions are the best form of advice

The presence of many 'co-coaches' in the group is one of the elements that can make group work so effective. When someone is stuck for an answer or very critical of themselves, there are others who can encourage, advise or share what they do that works. With any suggestion, it is important that what *might* be done does not turn into pressure on what *should* be done. This can be aided by turning a statement into a question which leaves a space for individuals to step into their own version. For example:

- That worked for me; if you were to think of doing something like that yourself, how would you go about it?
- If that wouldn't work for you, what do you think would be best for you at the moment?

It is also desirable to expand the 'question asking' repertoire of students. For example, a group of six 14-year-old boys with attendance and behaviour issues, asked each other in pairs: 'What small signs of progress have you been pleased to notice?' Key questions to follow this up were written on the board: 'How did you get that to happen?' and 'What made others proud of you?' Paired work can be especially supportive for quieter students who might find it easier to contribute when there is only one other person listening. The group were then brought together to 'report back'. During the final session with the same group of Year 9 boys, there was a group discussion about 'useful questions' and their suggestions were written on a board.

- What's better?
- How did you do that?
- How was that good for you?
- What was it that made you want to do it?
- What has been the effect on others around you?

The group then became a team of 'solution detectives' (Sharry et al. 2012) as each member of the group, in turn, was asked questions. For example, one boy said that he was pleased that since last time 'I've saved money'.

Group:	How did you do that?
Student:	By not spending on things I don't need, like extra food.
Group:	How was that good for you?
Student:	I don't get an upset stomach and so I don't need to go to the bathroom in the night.
Group:	What has been the effect on others around you?
Student:	They aren't disturbed by me flushing the toilet which is very loud!

This sequence is an example of the 'ripple effect' of SF questions: how the student ends up talking about changes in areas of their lives they – and maybe we – could not have predicted.

60. Follow up sessions

In follow up sessions, students can be asked to comment on what has been better for themselves and also what they have noticed other members of the group doing. This highlights and reinforces desirable behaviours in the context of school and lessons outside of the group. It can also help create a solidarity between the group members based on good things rather than unacceptable behaviours. It is not unusual for one member of the group to report how another member has helped them 'when I was losing it' or how they had looked out for each other between sessions. On occasions, a staff member can also report any good news they have heard. Picking up on all the finer details of difference and pointing the way to the next signs of progress can be further accessed through the scale.

61. Points of practice to bear in mind

Building team work

The group context offers a unique opportunity for students to build their social and collaborative repertoire. Team work has relevance outside the group to class-based activities and potentially the world of work. As John Sharry points out, groups enable members to experience both *getting from* and *giving to* other people through their active participation (Sharry 2007). We need to think about ways to capitalise on this during group sessions.

Maximising student ownership

Optimising student's input around process and content will aid contributions and the potential impact of the work.

- *Process*: The clearer the ground rules, the easier it is to use them as a benchmark to discuss what is happening in the group process and identify anything that needs to change: 'We talked earlier about the importance of "respecting the views of others" and I wondered what we have now learned that might be helpful in this. How would this show?' or 'How well do you think this "respect" is going in the group? What is working? What else would we like to see?' Peer pressure can work in many ways, and helping it to work in *supporting* the group process makes sense.
- *Content*: This has to be of interest *and* be seen as possible by the participants. Contributions can be evaluated through questions such as: 'What difference would this make?', 'How would that be good for you?' or 'How possible do you think this is?'

How to deal with challenging remarks

Having two workers, when possible, can allow for useful reflections or ideas during and between group sessions. If a challenging or 'unhelpful' remark is made, the key principle is to retain a stance of curiosity. For example:

- Ask 'what else' – there may be another idea lurking there.
- Relate the comment back to the stated purpose of the group. For example, a Year 10 student commented that he would walk out of class as a 'strategy' for remaining in the school. On first hearing, this is not helpful. However, when asked the question: 'I am assuming you must have had a good reason for doing this in helping you to stay in the school and I am curious as to what this might be?', the student outlined how walking out of class would lead to less trouble than getting into a fight when someone was winding him up. This provided a great opening into a wider discussion with the group as a whole about the ways they had managed to reduce or avoid trouble. Immediately after the final group session, this same student waited until the rest of the group had left before producing a box of chocolates from the pocket of his blazer. He mumbled 'Thanks Miss' as he too ambled off down the corridor!
- If necessary, students can be talked with outside of the group. In one Year 7 group, which was co-run by the practitioner and a support teacher, it had been very difficult to facilitate the first session due to silly and distracting comments. Prior to the second session, the support teacher running the group arranged a 10 minute individual discussion with each student. The purpose of the group, what would tell the student it had been useful and some expectations around behaviour were all explored. The students were also asked how we, the adults, would know that they were making the most of the group opportunity and what would be helpful if they were finding something difficult.

The conversations made a huge difference to the student's engagement in subsequent group discussions and they noticeably began to support each other inside and outside of the sessions. After the final session, the students sent a request to the head teacher to continue the group. The letter they wrote provided a further opportunity to think about how to present themselves and their arguments in a persuasive manner. A further six sessions were granted. The group went on to represent the school at a conference and the head teacher received many complimentary comments.

If a student can't answer a question

As mentioned previously, if a student can't think of a response, the discussion can move on, with the possibility of returning later in the session if they subsequently mention something which could be highlighted. When it is very hard to think, bringing in the perspective of others can also help. For example, 'What would your friends say they have noticed you doing in class which means you are not being asked to leave?'

62. Group mediation

The following case study (Ajmal 2006) looks at a session with two groups of Year 10 girls following a major fight which had resulted in three fixed term exclusions (with thanks to Evan George for his help in shaping this session).

It was agreed that a deputy head teacher would attend the session to help manage the process. There were 19 girls altogether including the excluded pupils who were to be escorted into the session and then off the premises again. One of these students was late. As she entered the already tense room, the student planted an air kiss next to everyone on one side of the room in turn, before ostentatiously turning her back on the other half and sitting down. It was hardly a manoeuvre out of the United Nations handbook.

Acknowledgement

Although the students had been *required* to attend the session, there are many shades of co-operation and students themselves are best placed to determine their own deluxe version. So I began by thanking the girls for coming and acknowledged that, while some of them may have been somewhat sceptical about how useful the session would be, the fact that they had come showed the school they were taking things seriously. It was also made very clear that no-one would be forced to say anything – it was up to the students to talk about the things they felt comfortable with and that they would be happy for the deputy head teacher to hear.

Warm-up activity

It can be useful to think about a warm-up activity to help a flow of conversation in a neutral context, for example, asking groups to discuss the worst celebrity outfit that week. The facilitator is best placed to judge whether this, or just getting on with it, is the best course.

Establishing a common direction

There were too many students to go around asking each one for their 'best hopes from the meeting'. Instead, a scale of 'How much do you want things to change?' was used where 10 represented a lot and 0 was not being bothered either way (i.e. they were happy with the way things were). Whilst the girls might have had different ideas at this stage about the specifics of who or what they wanted to change, if *none* of the students were happy with the way things were then that would have provided a shared starting point. Each student was asked in turn to give a number. The range was 1–8 and the collective list of good reasons behind the numbers included 'taking my studies seriously', 'not wanting bad reports to go home' and 'being fed up of being afraid to walk around the school on my own'. If anyone had stated a 0, they could still have been asked for the 'good reasons' behind their position and given the option to contribute if they felt they had something useful to say.

Agreement in the preferred future

'Strictly speaking it is a mistake to see the client's description of the preferred future as a "solution". More accurately, it is an alternative way of living in which the presenting issues have no significant part' (Ratner et al 2012: 93).

In small groups, the students were invited to:

- 'Imagine it is the Monday after half term and things have indeed changed in a way that is good for you and good for others'. The focus on 'good for you and good for others' encouraged a preferred future picture that involved them all.
- List what they, other students and school staff would be noticing. Identifying what others will witness adds increasing texture to the future that is wanted. It opens up the possibility that views can change or at least people would see something different.

As each group fed back one or two of their ideas, agreement emerged between all the girls that any attempts by the boys to start a rumour that could lead to a fight would not work. Some of the details were extended using questions such as: 'How would that show?' or 'What would be a sign of that?' A key point of difference for many of the girls was that they would all be 'happier and smiling at each other rather than scowling'.

Ownership cannot be forced

In the final activity, the girls were asked to: 'Imagine it is the end of the first week after the half term break and things have indeed been better for all of you. Looking back, what will you be remembering you had done that was helpful in this?' However, although a few ideas did emerge, much of what was said had been accessed in the previous question. When one student rightly commented, 'We are saying the same things', it was time to stop the conversation. The intention had been to introduce a subtle way of encouraging the girls to think about what they could actively do. However, the desire to formulate an action plan is far less effective than trusting the process and the students' own expertise about the situation and themselves. By avoiding goal-setting, the preferred future is left with more suppleness. The session ended with thanking the group for their contributions and acknowledging their capacity to do themselves justice in difficult circumstances.

What happened

On my next visit to the school a form tutor reported that things had been a lot calmer since the mediation session. Difference should be owned rather than imposed. Thus, when I bumped into two of the girls, I asked: 'What's been better?' rather than rushing into an enthusiastic restatement of what I had heard from the tutor.

Girl A:	Oh, they are much better now. There are no problems. We are friends now.
YA:	How come?
Girl B:	Well, when we left the meeting thing, someone remembered what you said about smiling (*this was an interesting attribution as 'smiling at each other' had come from the girls themselves*). Well, when we got out of the room someone said we have to smile and did this really funny smile. Someone else did another one and we burst out laughing. And it got us talking.

SFP is about constructing changes in people's lives and building a narrative that fits with the likelihood of further change. The idea of smiling and talking, initially stated as an indication of progress, was now a current success and remained a potential for a successful future. About a year later there was a further incident involving a small number of girls, a couple of whom had been in the mediation group the year before. I was asked to facilitate another mediation session. This time I met with each group of girls separately to ascertain their ideas about what might be helpful. One of the girls who had attended the meeting the previous year was present.

Student:	Are you going to make us have one of those meeting things again like we did last year?
YA:	Maybe. What I am interested in is what ideas you have about what might be helpful.
Student:	Well, I am not going to a meeting again … I mean it was good because it helped get us talking … but I won't do it again even if they make me.
YA:	Ok. So, what ideas do you have about what might be a good thing to try this time around?
Student:	Well, actually, it was good to get us to talk again. Maybe we could do some-thing like go to Nandos (a popular restaurant) and then we can talk and eat!

The girls did meet, eat and talk. More importantly, they also listened and both groups moved on sufficiently to warrant no further mediation input.

Parent groups

Bringing together groups of parents in schools provides a forum for them to share stories of success, to learn about their own strengths and to think of how their family life could be better in the future. Moreover, it is surprising how much good advice parents can give themselves and each other. The following section explores how SF questions can be used to help the 'best' version inside each parent to emerge. The ideas discussed could equally be used in individual discussions with parents.

63. Starting and finishing from a position of strength

Openings

The facilitator can ask everyone at the *beginning* of the first session to share an example of something that has gone well in their family life or a time when they had been at their best over the past few weeks. Parents can also get to know each other by asking: 'What would your family or best friend say they like about your child? What have you done to help build this quality?'

Endings

At the *end* of a session participants can be invited to comment on themselves, for example, something they have been reminded they do that is helpful or something they are proud of; or give feedback to each other, for example, saying a quality they have discovered or admire in the person on their left.

Parent skills

Sometimes asking parents to list their parenting attributes can help them to find their own foundation for moving forwards. In a group of parents of children with SEND (Special Educational Needs and Disabilities), pairs were asked to quiz each other to find 'at least 20 skills and qualities you bring to your parenting'. The skills were explored through different routes:

- *Different perspectives*: What they would say or what their family and friends would say.
- *Different contexts*: Breaking down the day into mornings, evenings, etc.
- *Different activities*: For example, homework or friendships. The activities can be generated by the parents.

If we never open the treasure chest, how can we know the delights that lie within. After the initial look of horror on the face of the parents in the group, in disbelief that there could possibly be 20 things to find, I was subsequently chastised for stopping the activity too soon! Many of the parents commented that the day-to-day demands of caring for their children rarely afforded time to step back to reflect on themselves and what they were doing. In response, I could not resist the temptation to ask: 'What difference has this reflection made?' An affirmation of the way they currently went about things had increased these parents' confidence in tackling things in the future. The accumulation of small details on a list, collectively, can pack a big punch.

64. Exploring what parents want

Asking parents 'What are your best hopes from attending this group?' helps to clarify, from the outset, what is of most significance. It can provide a focus for other questions and also helps parents to be clearer about what to listen out for. For example, in a group looking at the transition from primary to secondary school, parents were variously interested in ideas about how to prepare their children, how to manage their own anxiety and how to talk with their children about how things are going. Once established, questions such as: 'Suppose you are at your best in supporting your child in their move to secondary school?' 'What will you and they notice?' made sense at an individual level. Small mini interviews can then be conducted in rounds where each person offers a couple of ideas in turn. Alternatively, parents can be asked to talk to each other in pairs with some guiding questions.

If a parent states an issue such as: 'I am feeling very anxious' as the starting point, there would be a curiosity about what they would be feeling or doing *instead* when this has been resolved. Feeling anxious might translate for one parent into keeping themselves calm, and for another parent into making sure that their child did not pick up on their anxiety. The very act of moving a description from a current problem to what is desired can start the move towards solution talk and solution ideas.

Using scales

Scales can subsume seemingly disparate hopes under a more thematic umbrella. In one group, parents (all were mothers) asked each other scale questions in pairs about managing difficult situations with their children, which had been a common thread running through all the hoped-for changes. They were asked to think about their current number, useful things they had already discovered and what else they might be discovering over the next few weeks. The mothers were then asked to finish each mini interview with compliments to each other. The wheels of these short interviews were oiled by a short demonstration at the beginning so the parents could see the process in action. Subsequent meetings focused on what progress each person had seen, and how they had dealt with set-backs.

65. Being at our best

'Being at our best' or considering 'the best version possible' is a motivating and affirming way to help parents to reflect on the challenges they are facing. It assumes resourcefulness whilst at the same time taking account of the toughness of the situation.

A group of parents, whose children were transferring from the Special Educational Needs statementing process to the newly instigated Education, Health and Care Plans (EHCP), were meeting together. The journey through difficulties, diagnosis and fighting for your child can erode a sense of competence and future in parents and they were understandably anxious about what this change would mean. The first part of the session examined the proposed changes and what these would look like in practice. The second part of the session was spent helping the parents to build a picture of success in navigating themselves and their families through these changes and the plethora of professional meetings they would be attending. In groups, parents were asked to consider:

- Suppose you were to go into an EHCP meeting at your best, what will you notice?
- What would the professionals around the table notice about you?
- What will you be pleased to notice as you are raising difficult issues or when you don't agree with what is being suggested?

For some parents, their 'best' would emerge from the preparation they did before the meeting and clarity about the information they needed to find out. For other parents, it was about persisting in asking questions until they were clear about what was being proposed. This was less a set of actions and more a way for parents to build a sense of their own efficacy in supporting themselves and their children. At the end of the session, the parents had some ideas about the EHCP process and many more ideas about their own part in shaping what would be happening.

Interactive sequences

Being 'at your best' can also be an empowering position from which to think about constructive entry points into the 'action (I do this) – response (he does that) – action (I do this)' cycle of parent-child relationships. A group of parents of Year 11 students requested help from the school about how best to support their children in the run up to the exams. The first thing was to acknowledge the anxiety and worry most parents have at exam time and the tricky tightrope to walk between their children's desire for autonomy, pitched against their own knowledge garnered through experience and maturity. Despite their best intentions, what parents see as being helpful can equally be viewed as intrusive by their children. Parents were asked to describe themselves at their best in finding a fit between their child, the school work and themselves as parents. Using interactional questions, the parents built descriptions of how they would approach their son or daughter, how their son or daughter might respond and how they, at their best, might respond in turn. As one parent commented, this freeze-framing had helped her to consider the relative merits of certain responses and the value of paying attention to the nuances of a response that is often hidden under a fringe or a scowl. One parent, who was also the chair of governors at the school, reported to the head teacher that the session had been of immense value to her and, by extension, her son, and she had left with a renewed sense of confidence.

66. Advice giving

There can be a risk of someone in the group becoming the 'expert', which, in turn, can lead to the retort 'Oh, that wouldn't work for me' or 'Tried that!' What we want to do is to encourage a range of ideas that leaves each individual with the autonomy to select the idea that most fits with their situation and way of doing things.

In a very moving session with parents of children with life-threatening conditions, one parent talked about her difficulties in coming to terms with this. As the parents empathised and shared their own reflections, one parent described how he would imagine a time in the future when his son was no longer with him. And he imagined what he would be thinking at that time about what he had done while his son had been alive that would give him the greatest sense of pride and that his son would have most appreciated. When the original parent shared her own reflections, she referred to this idea and the sense of immediate comfort she had felt despite her pain and distress. These two parents continued to meet and talk after the group.

When parents ask 'What would you do?' or 'What should I do?', experience has taught that it is worth spending a few minutes exploring the ideas and thoughts that they are already bringing to the table. This is not to negate the proffering of advice. It is more a case of finding the balance, as a facilitator, between helping parents search for their own resources and making suggestions. For example, a group of parents of children in the early years asked how they could support their child's learning at home. Taking every day activities such as cooking and tidying up, parents in small groups were asked to list potential learning opportunities. They found sorting, counting, racing using a timer and turn-taking all within the auspices of tidying. Cooking occupied more technical territory with exploring textures, heavier and lighter and how heat changes food substances. Having involved parents in the process of generating their own ideas, they left the room with a greater probability of turning their hand to building learning into any home activity.

References

Ajmal, Y. (2006) Solution Focused Mediation in Schools. *Solution News* 2 (1): 3–6.

Metcalf, L. (1998) *Solution Focused Group Therapy*. New York: Simon & Schuster.

Ratner, H., George, E. and Iveson, C. (2012) *Solution Focused Brief Therapy: 100 Key Points and Techniques*. London: Routledge.

Ratner, H. and Yusuf, D. (2015) *Brief Coaching with Children and Young People: A Solution Focused Approach*. London: Routledge.

Sharry, J. (2nd ed., 2007) *Solution-Focused Groupwork*. London: Sage.

Sharry, S., Madden, B. and Darmody, M. (2nd ed., 2012) *Becoming a Solution Focused Detective*: *A Strengths-based Guide to Brief Therapy*. London: Routledge.

Young, S. (2009) *Solution-Focused Schools: Anti-bullying and Beyond*. London: BT Press.

Part 6 Creative adaptations for younger children

67. Noticing and naming

SF conversations fit well with the natural exploration of younger children as they learn about their worlds through trial, error and practical experience. As children begin to describe and share the good things they are learning about themselves, we can help them to highlight, magnify and attach significance to what they are doing. Once these behaviours have surfaced, we can then pay attention to keeping them afloat.

Smiley moments

A Year 2 teacher was concerned about the volume of negative comments from children in her class. A core of bright children would continually put down the contributions of others, particularly the less able and less confident children, which effectively silenced them during class discussions. Additionally, there were so many problems coming in from the playground that it was often difficult to settle them quickly back into learning. The teacher wanted to build a classroom environment where everyone felt safe and had the space to contribute. The achievement of every desired outcome begins with a first step: the step identified for these children was to practice and experience the art of saying and doing nice things.

Drawing on the principles of the WOWW approach (Berg and Shilts 2005), the practitioner was introduced to the class as someone who was interested in the good things that were happening. With clipboard in hand, particular attention was paid to times when a child said something nice to another child or did something kind, as these were the behaviours the teacher was most interested in seeing more of. At the end of 20 minutes, the observations were fed back. One of the children commented that the teacher was smiling as she was listening, so it was decided that 'smiley moments' would become their symbol for good things happening. This began a process where the children started to see themselves and the class differently. The teacher provided opportunities for 'smiley moments' to become a recurrent feature in the classroom. For example, asking children to feedback something their 'talk partner' had done that had made them smile or asking children as they returned from the playground: 'Who or what made you smile outside today?'

Within the security of this repetition, comments began to be initiated by the children themselves. Whenever the practitioner visited the class, the students would immediately start to recount something kind they had done, or a 'smiley moment' someone had given them. In the early stages, some of the quieter students benefitted from encouragement to contribute and some statements needed a little reshaping, for example, 'I helped Sandy in the playground because no one likes to play with her'! However, it set a tone and with persistence, more and more complimentary comments began to surface. As their expertise grew, so did the variety and complexity of the 'smiles' the children were describing.

What the teacher had to say about 'smiley moments'

The teacher commented on the marked change in the confidence and contributions from the more vulnerable children in the class. Other children now listened to their views and they were more likely to be included into group activities. In fact, three of the quietest students had recently devised and delivered a little quiz about the Fire of London topic the class were studying. This had put them in the rare position of being in charge and the whole class had joined in and supported them. There had also been a significant reduction in complaints and upset from children as they returned from playtime. Instead, there were 'smiley moment' comments about children being asked to join in a game or being helped when they fell over.

The teacher also felt that the work with the class had provided experience in, and evidence for, some of the school's key strategic criteria in raising the voice of the child. For example, building empathy, building emotional intelligence and helping children to begin to see things from others' points of view. Fundamentally, however, the project had reinforced what the children were already doing.

> I am not saying that these things never happened before, but they were not noticed. Highlighting and bringing things to the forefront has helped, because the children can see and aspire to be someone that people admire. These are only small things and yet they have made a big difference. It saves a teacher's energy and it is a happier classroom. It has also been fun.
>
> (Sophia Charles, class teacher)

Videos - helping students to 'catch themselves being good'

Using a video can facilitate a closer examination of what is happening. Slowing down the process by playing short sections of the video enables the minutiae of details to emerge and gives a context for further questions such as: 'How did you *do* that?' or 'What happened when you did that?' The more dynamic the descriptions and the more they are added to over time, the more control younger children will feel as they practice shaping and reshaping their skills.

A teacher asked for some help with two students, Carly and Baleegh, who were finding it difficult to work with others in the classroom and did not particularly like each other. The teacher wanted Carly and Baleegh to find ways of working collaboratively. They were given the task of building a bridge together out of newspaper and sticky tape, and the 10 minute session was videoed. Looking at the video together to find examples of 'good working together' was a challenge as the pair had worked largely side by side with virtually no interaction. However, there were small elements of behaviour that could be commented on, such as handing each other the sticky tape or waiting until the other had finished before taking it. These behaviours could easily have been overlooked and yet in noticing them, they were available again to be elaborated on. Carly and Baleegh were then asked to observe two other children building a bridge together and to write down all the things *they* were doing well. They enjoyed their position of 'expertise' in this task and more interactions could be observed as Carly and Baleegh compiled their list together. In doing so, they were also adding to their own profiles of what 'good working together' looked like in practice.

A couple of weeks later, Carly and Baleegh were again filmed completing another problem-solving activity. What a difference! They listened more to each other's ideas, checked out what they were doing and made nice comments. At the end of the activity, Carly and Baleegh were asked what they had noticed and appreciated about each other:

> Baleegh: I like working with Carly. She really gets me and how I do things.
>
> Carly: Baleegh has really good ideas and if there is a problem he can come up
>   with some solutions.

5 minute observations

Five minute 'on the spot' observations could also be carried out by children who are unsettled and might need help in getting back on track. By being asked to pick out some of the good things they can see happening in the class, they might also draw inspiration from the other children in finding at least some of their own solutions to whatever the issue is. Any feedback from these observers could be supported by questions such as:

- What was your favourite thing?
- Can you (insert observation)?
- Show me your way of (insert observation).
- If you had to teach someone else to (insert observation), what would you say or do?

68. Keeping good things going

The more children pay attention to an action or a behaviour, the more real it becomes and the more likely it is that they will start creating the scenarios that they are describing. There are many ways that conversations about the good things that are happening in a classroom can be developed:

- The children's ideas can be recorded on displays, on a list at the front of the classroom, in a special book or in a specially named box to serve as a reminder of all that is good in the class.
- A scale-type gauge could be used to look at how good things have been in relation to whatever the class are paying attention to, for example, 'Where are we on the "kind-ometer" today?' The number, whether low or high, is a gateway into useful details about what has occurred.
- Monitors can be appointed to carry out short observations or the help of 'Bertie the Helpful Bear' can be called upon to help notice the good things that are happening.
- Changing the emphasis very slightly can prolong the appeal for much longer. For example, having a focus for the week such as 'good things in the playground' or 'good things in helping each other'.
- Younger children can draw a picture of the good things they are seeing or someone can act as a scribe. Asking children to draw something that 'made them smile' in the playground as they come in from the outside can also help to calm transitions.
- Photographs taken showing 'moments' when the class are working well together or asking children to draw a picture of 'your best moment in our best lesson', can be made into a book for future reference.
- For the very young, 'good or happy moments' could become embedded in the classroom through physical activities such as a 'Happy Chair' where children can elect to sit and talk about the things that had made them 'happy' that day.

When other people notice the good things

Someone showing an interest, such as the head teacher or another significant adult, can also be powerful in supporting more lasting changes. Popping their head around the door every so often, the adult can enquire about four good things that have been happening or even asking the class to give them a 'smiley moment' to cheer them up. Even if the children have not been thinking about good things up to that point, the very fact of asking will bring the idea back into their minds.

69. Co-creating pictures of success: children as experts

Seeing and doing is often a more relevant way for younger children to build a picture of success than words alone. A Year 2 teacher wanted to pay attention to the children working together in a supportive way, so that *their* ideas about what this would look like were brought to the fore. Seeing something in action and being given the opportunity to describe what is happening can help younger children build their repertoire of what they do.

Modelling

An activity was set up where the teacher and a teaching assistant initially modelled working together on a 'squiggle drawing'. This involves two people with a different colour pen. Each person carries out a small part of the drawing in turn, swapping over and back again until the drawing is declared finished or time runs out.

In the first attempt, the teacher and teaching assistant told the class they were 'finding it hard' to work together. However, they were aided by 30 'working together experts'. Every time there was a difficulty (such as snatching, not handing over the drawing, making unpleasant comments), a hypothetical 'pause button' was pressed and the 'experts' were asked for some ideas. This could equally well be a red stop sign or any other representation. At one point, when the teacher and teaching assistant were starting to squabble, one of the children said: 'Quick, push the pause button because they need our help'. The children loved to see their teachers in the role of learners and stepped naturally into their role of 'helpers'.

The fruits of the children's teaching were then witnessed by a second attempt at a squiggle drawing where the teacher and teaching assistant practiced the art of negotiation and co-operation based on the children's suggestions: 'Shall I start or do you want to start?' or 'That's a nice line there, do you mind if I add a bit on here?' Every so often the activity was stopped and the children were asked to compliment their teacher and the teaching assistant on what they noticed or liked about the way they were working together.

Being open to detours and developments

Sometimes children can take us by surprise, and it is important to keep a genuine openness to what they bring. The teacher noticed that pairs of children squiggle drawing together had been using more than two colours. This had not been the intention of the activity nor had it been discussed. The teacher was about to talk to the children about not following instructions when she decided instead to ask them what had happened. From the responses she received, the teacher learnt that the class had spontaneously taken the squiggle activity one step further by negotiating sharing the colours between pairs. Afterwards the teacher commented: 'I realise that when children are given a structure and involved in thinking about how to help each other, they take responsibility for developing their own ideas'.

The children's behaviour so inspired the teacher that she decided to set up a 'whole class squiggle drawing' where the 30 6- and 7-year-olds collectively drew on one huge piece of paper in the corridor. The activity provided a great opportunity to ask the children for their own ideas about the logistics of getting 30 artists out of the classroom and into the corridor to draw on one huge length of paper:

- How will you decide who goes where? ('The boys could go on one side and the girls on the other'.)
- Who will do what? ('We can talk together and see if we want to draw with someone or on our own'.)

Potential sticking points can also be addressed through 'What if?' questions and the adults can always add in their ideas:

- What will you do if you want a colour that someone else has? ('We will say to them "Can I borrow that colour please?"')

- And if they are still using it? ('We will wait until they have finished'.)
- What if someone is upset? ('We will ask what's wrong and help'.)

What the children had to say about the class squiggle drawing

When the teacher asked the children to write about the experience, among the many comments she received were the following, presented as in their original versions:

- *About how they worked together*: 'I watied pashentleey for my pen to come back'.
- *About how they helped each other*: 'At ferst I was shiy then my friend cam over and sed don't wiry I will sit with you for a lit ell wiyall'.
- *About how much fun they had had*: 'I felt like it was the best day of my life'.

Seeing the whole class working together, being the best version of themselves they could be, was quite breathtaking. Three children, without being asked, had helped a child with a diagnosis of autism to join in and when, half way through the activity, the teacher moved every alternate child to a different position, there was a seamless continuation of the drawing.

70. Other ideas to help scaffold 'noticing' and 'doing'

Using activities to build skills and confidence

Activities that are fun and of relevance can be inserted anywhere in the school day and used as a basis for building the confidence and skills of the children. For example, using problem solving tasks such as lining up from the smallest to the tallest child can help build children's skills in talking, listening and working together. The 'dig deeper' feature of SFP can then help children to pay attention to and name what they did, how they did it, what others did and any other good ideas they have. The smaller and more visible actions are, the more likely they are to be used again.

A Year 3 class were divided into groups and asked to line up in order of 'who has the shortest to the longest hair' without talking. One of these groups was comprised of five boys all of whom found it hard to settle to activities with other children and would quickly reject work they were finding challenging. It also happened that every one of the boys had very short hair and thus it was a demanding task. What was impressive was how the boys stuck with the activity until they had ordered themselves, even though the rest of the class had finished and were sitting in their groups. This was as astonishing as it was unexpected and offered a different view of the boys to themselves, the class and their teacher. The boys were asked to comment on all the small things they had done that had helped them to work it out and keep going. They talked about carrying on thinking of good ideas and trying things out. Successes such as these can provide reference points in the future when something difficult is encountered: gently talking with the boys about the time when they did the 'line up' and all that was useful then.

71. Stepping into the world of imagination

The most compelling conversations with young children are fun. Their imagination is a gift that can stretch our own creativity in finding ways of talking with them. Looking at the best things can be, what they are already doing and ways they can make progress can all be informed by the natural inventiveness of young children.

Show me how

Chris Iveson has written about working with a 5-year-old boy who said that for things to be happier in school he should not run in class. Asked what he would do instead, he said 'walk'. At Chris's invitation, the boy showed off his considerable walking skills. They then engaged in a role play where Chris became the boy and the boy took the role of the teacher so that he could 'teach' Chris 'what was required of him as the child!' (Ratner et al. 2012: 175–176).

Role playing

When working as a teacher in a tough inner London primary school, I (YA) was struggling to work out how I would manage a class of bubbly reception children in the less structured environment of the end of term party. During story time a few weeks prior to the party, a child wanted to know what 'lords and ladies' (mentioned in the story) did. So, we practiced bows and curtseys and 'please' and 'thank you'. The class party, to which lords and ladies were invited, was a most civilised affair. After the party, questions such as: 'How would a lord ask for the football?' continued to provide a context to think about what to do and how to do it.

In younger classes, teachers can set up a 'sorting out' area filled with various props such as packs of the key characters from stories, small world people, persona dolls, etc. Children can then re-enact stories or create their own versions to add layers to their understanding. They can be given prompts such as: 'What can you do to help mouse find a friend?' (Carle 1987). Therese Steiner has also written about the use of puppets to help children find their voice, talking through the puppet as it were.

> When you work with hand puppets, you must remember one thing ... talk to the puppet and not to the child. This is very important because it helps children to stay in the role of the animal (puppet) ... they choose at a safe distance from themselves, while at the same time experiencing parts of their own behaviour or the behaviour they will strive for in the future.
>
> (Berg and Steiner 2003: 78)

A younger child could also be asked to imagine they are a superhero with a 'power' that they can use in the classroom or with their group. It might be useful to have an initial short discussion about what the power is, followed by what it would look like in specific activities such as getting their books out, working at their table, helping someone else or whatever aspect the teacher might like to highlight with the child. The child could then be instructed to: 'Start using your power this morning and let's see if the children can guess what it is'.

Language

The more children are exposed to the language of SF, the more this is likely to have an influence on how they talk to each other. Stories provide a natural entrée into a world of possibilities:

- Catchy phrases, such as: 'I want ...' from the books by the same name (e.g. Ross 2017), can be built on to help children think about aspirations they have for themselves.
- *Have you filled your bucket today?* (McCloud and Messing 2016) can provide the opportunity for children to say and do nice things to fill the buckets of all the children in the class.
- A child playing 'Max' from *Where The Wild Things Are* (Sendak 2013) can sit on the hot seat and the teacher can ask: 'What did you do to tame the wild things?' This can help children to think about what they do to help themselves and others calm down.
- Songs, rhymes or anything with a repetitive aspect can also be used. For example, 'I went to the playground and I (action)', used as a round where each child can add the action they will do when they are playing nicely in the playground.

Star moments, sparkle shakes, bucket fillers all provide the opportunity for children to explore, use and share ideas. Imagine the surprise of a Year 5 teacher approached by a Year 3 child in the playground who said: 'I am giving my sparkle to Leanne because she helped me up when I fell over'. Her Year 3 class had not been working with 'sparkles', yet, somehow, they had spread via the natural absorbency of children.

72. One-to-one conversations

Pace and ownership

The more we use the child's own experiences and expressions, the more likely they are to be able to identify with and engage in the things we are talking about. The more we go at their pace and listen out for their openings, the more likely it is that we will be walking alongside them rather than trying to nudge them in a particular direction.

Joe, 7 years old, had joined his school a few months earlier, having been permanently excluded from his previous school. He was struggling with his learning and behaviour which was not helped by a fragmented pattern of attendance. Despite having a good relationship with his teaching assistant (Mrs Day) and class teacher (Mr Stanley), Joe refused to talk about his behaviour and would become angry and upset if he felt he was being forced to do so. The practitioner was asked to work with Joe and Mrs Day to find a way of talking with him about what was happening.

The session began with asking Joe to draw a scale on a piece of paper and he decided that the 10 was to be 'the best as ever' and 0 was to be 'the worst as ever'. Although he was rarely known to sit down and write anything, during the next 10 minutes he painstakingly sounded out and wrote the words at the top and bottom of the scale. His writing was interspersed with short discussions about the respective merits of the two pens we were using and a repetitive checking that their tops fitted. However, he continued until he had finished and held the writing up for inspection. Although this activity took much longer than anticipated, through the act of drawing and writing, the scale became Joe's scale and this was significant to his engagement in the rest of the conversation.

When things are difficult, it is natural to forget about the better times, and yet they can be a fertile ground for inspiration. Rather than asking Joe to rate where things were currently, the practitioner opted to find out what number he would put for when things *had* been at their best in school. A simpler version for a younger child could be to ask about something that had made them or their teacher happy. Joe reported that during his first week at the school, things would have been as high as a 9. Among the details about what was happening at the 9, Joe included 'sitting up' and 'being helpful'. He then mumbled: 'And I wasn't doing them tantrum things'. The very fact that Joe mentioned the *absence* of tantrums meant he was, of course, giving recognition to this behaviour. Mrs Day commented after the session that this was the first time Joe had even hinted that this was what was happening.

Given the opening Joe had provided, the track that was pursued was one of competence: 'What did you do instead of the tantrums? How did you manage to do that?' The desired behaviour is one where no tantrums reside. Joe talked with some passion about 'squashing the niggles'. His best method for this was smiling and helping, both of which he was able to demonstrate with gusto. 'Niggles' then became the metaphor for the rest of the conversation as can be shown with this extract:

Practitioner:	What if that 'niggle' really, really, really wants to niggle you?
Joe:	I don't know. I will just stop it.
Practitioner:	You will just stop it?
Joe:	Like that. (*clicks fingers*)
Practitioner:	Just like that? (*I click my fingers; rather poorly as it is a skill I don't actually have*)
Joe:	One click and it's gone. (*several finger-clicks and smiles*)
Practitioner:	And if Mrs Day sees you do that clicking, what will that tell her?
Joe:	That the 'niggle' has gone. (*clicks*) See, they're gone.

After role-playing how to deal with 'persistent niggles', Joe drew a 'niggle scale' which he elected to run from 0–100, where 100 was 'no niggles' (being happy and smiling) and 0 was lots of niggles. Joe added a '50' halfway along the scale and so he was asked what would be happening at a 50. Joe talked about 'being a bit helpful and then a bit with niggles'. He then started zooming up and down the scale: 'Weeee down – niggle – click – up again – down with the niggles – click – up again'. This was more than playing, Joe was actually getting the sense of his own agency in moving between the 0 and 100.

The conversation ended with Joe filming the practitioner asking Mrs Day what she knew about Joe that made him such a 'niggle squashing expert'. Joe heard himself described as 'determined' and 'someone who has lots of good ideas'. Mrs Day commented that having a way of talking with Joe about his behaviour gave her and the school greater confidence that they could all work with him and find a way forward.

'Coming out of' rather than 'going in'

A teacher wanted some help in working with a 5-year-old boy, Andy, who was having huge tantrums in her class when he met with something difficult. These could continue for a considerable length of time. Any attempt to unpick what had led to the tantrum was met with silence and shrugs, and the ideas she herself had about what had caused the tantrums were not leading to any progress. Tantrums, however, have entry points and exit points. So, *after* the tantrum was over, the teacher began to talk with Andy about his strengths and skills at calming himself down – what he did and how he did it. Some of his ideas were described in words, others in drawings or 'showing'. The conversations were about success and competence and over time a picture emerged of a boy who could control rather than be controlled by the tantrum. Eventually, the teacher began to talk with Andy about what he did that was helpful when he felt a tantrum 'creeping up'. After the first few conversations, most of these dialogues took place in 5 minute slots. Five years later, when Andy was one of the oldest students in the school, he devised a series of stories which he would show, using stick puppets, to some of the younger children. The central character was a clever boy who knew how to beat tantrums.

References

Berg, I.K. and Shilts, L. (2005) Keeping the Solutions inside the Classroom. *ASCA School Counsellor*, July/August.

Berg, I.K. and Steiner, T. (2003) *Children's Solution Work*. New York: W.W. Norton.

Carle, E. (1987) *Do You Want to Be My Friend?* New York: Harper and Collins.

McCloud, C. (2016) *Have You Filled Your Bucket Today?* Brighton, MI: Bucket Fillers.

Ratner, H., George, E., and Iveson, C. (2012) *Solution Focused Brief Therapy: 100 Key Points and Techniques*. London: Routledge.

Ross, T. (1993) *I Want to Be!* London: Anderson Press.

Sendak, M. (2013) *Where The Wild Things Are*. London: Red Fox.

Part 7 Case example of individual work

73. Transcript

Christiana is a Year 7 (first year secondary school, 12 years old) student who was sent to see the school counsellor (YA) for a 25 minute session. Permission had been given from her and her family to record the session, so the following is the transcript taken from the recording, with appropriate changes made to safeguard her confidentiality.

As soon as she enters the room, Christiana begins complaining about teachers and how she is on report but getting NA's (not achieved) for her various targets. Christiana then takes off her bag and sits back. I open with our routine opening question, regarding her hopes from the meeting.

Ok – so what are your best hopes from our meeting that would be most helpful to you in terms of your teachers?

I don't know. I don't like their classes and especially with French I want to move and I told her loads of times: 'Can I move to Spanish please?' Because I didn't bring my slip in for what language I wanted, so I had to go straight to French and didn't want to so …

She was moving into full flow so I attempt to gently interrupt by offering a simple closed question to show I am listening.

So you are having to go to a lesson that's not of your choosing, is that right?

Right. And the teacher she's always like …

And here the floodgates opened to a stream of complaints about the teacher, so I step in with another statement of acknowledgment. My hope is that if she thinks I am hearing her, she will be able to slow down and pay attention to some different and more constructive questions.

So you are finding her hard to get on with.

And then when a boy threw water at me, yeah, when it was hot, she said to Miss V, our head teacher, that I was in a water fight. I was throwing water at a boy, when he threw some water at me because he tried to get another boy and then he threw it at me and he said sorry. And I said: 'It's alright', because it was only a little bit and she went to Miss V and I had to go to an hour's detention – miss all my lunch …

Clearly I am going to have to come at this in a different way to capture her attention away from a detailed catalogue of what's happened to her!

Right, that doesn't sound like, from your point of view, that was very fair. So in terms of your French lesson – what's the best thing – what do you think we could do together today? What would you like us to do that might be helpful to you in dealing with that situation?

I don't know. If you could move me that would be good, but I don't suppose you can.

So if I wasn't able to do that, and we could talk about that in a moment if you like, if I wasn't able to do that, what would be your next best hopes from our meeting?

I don't know.

A second 'don't know'. Although I have not got a direction yet, it has definitely stopped her talking and started her thinking. I said that 'we could talk about that' because I am leaving open the option of returning to this topic if I have feel I have nowhere else to go in the conversation – not to suggest that I could do something for her but to explore questions such as: 'What difference would it make to you if you could move to Spanish?' For now, I plough on with a slightly different version of the 'best hopes' question and this time I do not manage to finish what I am asking before she answers.

So, if you walked out of this discussion and thought 'actually that was really helpful to me', any ideas of what ...

Just like ignore her and stuff. But the thing is, she's the only teacher I can't ignore. If another teacher turns around and says: 'Take your jacket off', they say it nicely. But she has got this thing about her she just says it horribly. That's why I get into a big strop.

It is tricky when a student blames others for their problems. I decide to treat this as a 'route' to change and through this lens see what possibilities emerge.

So you are finding things much more difficult. It sounds as if you have worked out some strategies for dealing with other difficulties.

They're 'safe', those teachers. But she's just ...

Can I just ask you – let's imagine for a minute that you were able to ignore her. What difference would that make to you if you found a way of doing that?

A big difference.

It would?

But I don't know how to ignore her. She just stares in your face, like she proper keeps on nagging you. Like the first time you see her, yeah, and you don't set a really good impression, she'll just take you on for the next 5 years in school.

Right. So you feel ...

She took it on for the next bloody year I am in this school. If I have her next year, oh my god.

So one of the things is that by the end of this year there might be a different teacher?

Even if there is a different teacher I still want to move to Spanish.

Yes, I can hear that.

You know, my dad, he's from Spain.

Yes ... that would make a big difference to you when you see your family there ...

'Cos I am going this summer.

Are you?

At least I'll be like – if I just move to Spanish now I'll be able to get a bit done at least.

Hmm. Can I just take you back to something you said a few minutes ago? You said if you could find a way of ignoring this teacher – you say it sounds unlikely at the moment, that it's going to be hard. You said it's going to make a BIG difference. Can you tell me a bit more about that 'big difference' it is going to make to you?

I'd just be able to get on with my work more. Miss L is just sitting writing things down. She sits behind me and basically if she weren't there, yeah, because if I thought ignoring her, seeing that she weren't there, it would just be so much better.

So you would be able to get on with your work?

Yeah. I'd be able to get on with my work, be able to have a little chat with my friends at the table next to me and all that.

So have a balance – you'd be able to get a good balance?

The word 'balance' hasn't come from her; strictly speaking I should have checked if she saw it that way herself.

But, like, I was writing on this little paper, just drawing, just scribbling, like, because the teacher was doing something on the computer and then she came and took it off me and wrote in my report 'Christiana was writing notes to other people' or something like that.

Again she feels driven to tell me more about what has bothered her and I have to ensure I don't get swept away by this. As you can see, I make a statement, check it out with her and then ask a question all in one go!

So it sounds like you would like to see yourself settling down to your work in that class. Have I heard you right? And if you did find yourself doing that, what difference would that make to you?

A BIG difference in my GCSEs because we have to have an end of term test in French and ... I've done quite well in science and maths so I am quite smart, but I don't know ...

So you'd find yourself being able to use that smartness more in French?

I doubt I'd be able to get a high level, I'd be really shocked. I don't like getting low levels.

How come?

I don't know. It's just, like, I won't really be comfortable getting a low level so ...

So what sort of level would you be aiming for in a subject like French, which is a newer subject, isn't it, for you?

Well the highest you can get is about a 4. The highest because it is a new thing to us. Or a 3. Most people get 3, but extremely clever people get 4, but I doubt that will be me because I don't concentrate in class because I can't, she's so ....

I respond to the part that is most closely aligned with possibilities for change.

Is that something you would like to see yourself getting?

Yeah.

You'd like to see yourself getting a 4?

Yeah.

Repetition of what sound like significant, constructive responses can help focus a student's mind.

How come?

I don't know, it will just be good for my record, innit? I'm one of these people who are quite bad but have a good, like, education. And I've got excluded four or five times in this school and I'm only in Year 7. Not even a lot of people in Year 10 have been excluded five times. Plus, if I get higher levels, yeah, I'd still be able to get a good job ...

So you're thinking of that - you're thinking about studying now for your future beyond school?

Yeah.

Ok.

Although this is some way off in the future, anything that is motivational is worth pursuing.

I want to have fun plus get on with my education.

Ok, that sounds like a good aim to have, so that you have things you enjoy and also you take your studying seriously. Is that what you are saying?

Yes

So, it sounds like you've done a lot of hard thinking now about the things you need to do to keep that option ...

But I doubt it because in primary, the reason I got high levels was because I learnt things. In this school, no matter which subject it is I don't learn that much. 'Cos basically when I was in 7A, like, before Christmas, our class was just so disruptive. That's why some people moved. Now in 7B, I used to think it was a little geeky class and when I came here we hardly get on with our work, no-one does. The teachers, if they are fed up with us they won't teach us. Basically, I think teachers should give us another try. I know if I was a teacher and I had little screaming people, children, in my class, I'd get really angry. That's why I am not going to be a teacher!

Right - you know that's not for you ...

Because I can't handle it. I don't know how teachers can!

So you said something very interesting about that you want to have fun. Is that right? And study?

Although fun would not be useful on its own, as part of a wider picture that also included study, it is worth exploring a little further.

Yeah.

What would that look like if you were doing that? What would tell you that you had got that balance really well from your point of view? What would you notice yourself doing?

Getting good grades - yeah. Getting good grades but also having a few friends. Not being bullied because I'd hate getting bullied.

So getting good grades ...

Yeah.

Having friends ...

Yeah.

Not being bullied ...

I doubt I'd be bullied but ...

Right, Ok.

Because I stick up for my friends, that's why they like me a lot.

So would that be something you would be doing? Sticking up for friends?

Yeah, but not like getting too much into their business. If they want to have beef with some girl, I'd back them up. If she got her girls, I'd back her up, my friend, but I wouldn't like jump in unless her friends jumped in, that other girl …

Friendship groups are crucially important to students. It would probably be pointless to try to argue against a friend sticking up for another friend; the key thing is how they can do that in a way that is best for all concerned - including the school.

And if you were managing to stick up for your friends in a way that was good for you and also good for your learning, how would you be doing that?

Outside school, of course.

Ok.

Like if I did it inside school then I'd be in bad trouble, but outside school …

So you would be clear about where you did it …

Yeah.

What else will you be doing that will tell you that you'd got the balance right, in terms of having fun in school and taking your studies seriously, so getting a good learning?

Not having fun in a bad way, like being in trouble. When you are in trouble, it's fun when you are doing the trouble but the consequences ain't fun, that's the thing.

That's a very good distinction!

Like when you are laughing about, yeah. When you are running around the school or playing in a water fight. I ain't done it in this school yet, but I probably will when it gets hotter and I'll end up getting a detention, but …

I ignore the unhelpful description and refocus on what is potentially useful.

So how could you have fun in a way that's not a bad way?

Just … a lot of people do it in this school and I don't see how they do it because, I don't know, because it's hard for me to be like a little goody goody and have fun. Because I have fun in classes and I can turn to my friends and then the teacher says: 'Be quiet', then I'm like, 'Oh, but we're not even chatting that loud'.

You say other people do it. You're not quite sure how they do it?

Yeah.

That's how you would like to do it?

But then I feel sorry for the people. I've got some people in my class who don't have fun at all. Some people bully them a bit. They study so hard to be clever but..

So, if we look at your French lesson just for a moment …

Very low!

… and you were having fun in your French lesson and also learning. If you were being true to what you want for yourself, what would that look like?

To me or the teacher?

That's a good question. Shall we say to you first and then have a look at the teacher afterwards?

To me, that would look like … do you mean having fun in a bad way or a good way?

In a way that is good for you. In a way that…

That I won't get into trouble?

Yeah.

And the teacher didn't mind me laughing or chatting?

Shall we just see what that would look like?

That would be the perfect lesson. But …

So what would that look like in French then? It's a hard one I know …

That would look like I've tried and the teachers have tried as well, so we are both trying to get on with each other. So …

Ok. If I could ask you a bit more about that, if I saw you trying, what would I see you do that would tell me that you were trying?

Sometimes it helps to evoke a fly-on-the-wall perspective. Christiana here elaborated on how hard she would work, how she would then 'have a little chat with my friend' and when the teacher told her to get on with her work, 'I'd say: "Alright sir"'.

So your thinking is that if you do your work and maybe even a bit extra, that would give you a bit of leeway?

Yeah.

That's a very interesting way of looking at it.

'Cos if say people ain't even finished the first sheet and I've done two sheets including the extra one, like three sheets, and they ain't even done the first sheet, then I am already ahead of them.

There was a knock at door, meaning the next student was waiting for their appointment. Time to end the session – 2 minutes left! I won't have time to examine the teacher's perspective, even though I said we would come to that.

So how would you feel about yourself … let's leave the teacher's view for now. How would you feel about yourself if you saw yourself getting on with the work, finishing the sheet, maybe having a little chat, doing an extra bit?

That's what the perfect school would be.

There's an implication here that this is an unrealistic picture. However, she has said so much about what is possible and her part in this that I endeavour to hold onto that.

And for yourself? How would you feel about yourself if you did that? Would it suit you to do that?

Yeah.

It would?

Because I would be getting high levels. Because I'd be doing the work I'd be getting a good comment from my teacher, that I'm doing all my work and I'd also be having a little chat at the same time.

So that sounds like the Christiana you would like to see yourself in school. And I'm guessing that to be able to tread that boundary takes some skills. I would imagine it would take somebody who was good at thinking and good at learning in order to be able to. Because I guess that some people misjudge it and it goes right over their heads.

Christiana nods and smiles

So, it's about getting the balance in the middle. I think that's really interesting. We're going to need to finish now, but would you like to come back again? I am back again next week. Would that be too soon or would that be a good time?

That would be a good time.

I'd like to think some more with you about getting that balance right ...

But it's ... I try but the teachers don't!

Ok. So maybe we can think about that and what you notice about teachers when they do try that makes a difference to you.

Yeah.

And you know what would be really interesting? Just notice the times when you do get that balance right for you whatever the teacher does. The times when you do get it right because it might be interesting to think about what you are doing at those times. That's a very interesting idea.

My use of the word 'balance' relates to our experience of working with those young people for whom it seems important not to give up on behaviours that adults are critical of for fear that, to use Christiana's words, they're seen as a 'goody goody'. For such students, the idea of staying close to the 'middle', as I called it, makes most sense – how to have fun and be 'good' in a way that's right for you and for the school.

In general, it's helpful to finish with some compliments to whoever we have been talking to and sometimes to add on a 'noticing task'. This is hardly a task in the usual sense of the word as they are only being asked to keep their eyes open, but it means that the last thing they hear from us is an idea of something constructive for them to focus on, and connects with our 'follow up' meeting with them. The first idea is to pay attention to when teachers do try as there would undoubtedly be examples of this that she has not picked up on. The second emphasis is to reiterate a focus on Christiana herself that was not dependent on teachers changing as the catalyst.

I saw Christiana a couple more times before the summer break and although by no means perfect, things were definitely more settled to such an extent that Christiana reported that she and the French teacher had become, in her word, 'friends'. I encouraged her to elaborate on what she had done, what she had learned from this and her confidence in keeping herself on the track that was right for her. An appointment was arranged for the new term (Year 8) in September, but Christiana and the school did not think it was needed.

74. How are reputations formed, maintained and changed?

At the beginning of the following spring term Christiana asked the school if she could speak to me again. Things had got a little rocky and she said with some passion:

> I haven't had a good couple of weeks and I keep hearing teachers say: "Oh, the old Christiana is back", when they forget that I have had a whole term when I have not been on report or in trouble.

In a sense, Christiana had a point. Once a view of someone or something has been established, it can become a default position from which it is difficult for people to move, and any attempts at difference are dismissed as temporary. On the other hand, some staff will wonder, when a student has a set-back, whether the SF approach meant that their 'real' or 'deeper' problems hadn't been 'dealt with'. There is obviously a chance, using any approach, that something crucial can be missed. We don't pretend that SF works 100%. But the life of every young person is filled with varying influences, ranging from 'internal' states to 'external' events and we think that it makes sense to start from the position that they are doing their best to deal with what life is throwing at them and for us to help them amplify their strengths and enable them to get back on track.

It sounds as though things are really tough at the moment. Can I ask you what might sound like an odd question?

Go on then.

Are things the worst that they have ever been?

To hear what the school is saying you would think that I was the worst student in the school. They just keep going on and on. And they won't listen when I try and tell them.

And from your point of view? How would you describe things?

Well, no. They are not as bad. God, if they really had the Year 7 Christiana back …

Ok. So things are not as bad as they have been. Hmm. How have you managed that? How have you stopped things from being worse?

This gives prominence to an intention to keep things away from the worst position rather than focus attention on what is causing things to spiral downwards. It gave Christiana the opportunity to describe those actions that were potentially useful rather than defend those actions that were not helpful. A list began to emerge of all the small things and big things that Christiana was doing such as keeping up with her work and choosing the friends that she was spending time with. As the list grew so Christiana began to calm down.

I then asked what Christiana's best hopes from this discussion were. There were many strands of enquiry possible and I wanted to make sure that the questions I asked would have the best fit with the desired outcome. Christiana wanted the school to back off and realise that she was doing things differently and to give her a chance when she didn't do everything perfectly. This led into some questions about what getting things back on track from her point of view and from the point of view of the school would look like.

Well, the school might notice that I was not getting into so many loud arguments with some of the teachers. The thing is that they don't listen and …

Hmm. So what would you and they notice instead?

(Pause) I don't know. If I have got something to say I am going to say it. I don't care what they think.

So that is important to you – to state your view. And what would you notice about the way you put your view across? That did justice to what you wanted to say and that the school would listen to?

I don't know. I mean I just tell them now ….

Christiana found this a difficult question. So I asked her to pick a teacher and imagine a situation when she had something to say. And then I invited her to describe, step by step, what she would be thinking, saying and doing. Although this might sound like a similar conversation to the one Christiana and I had been having in the Year 7 session, it was important that my questions were open to the differences that began to be more evident as Christiana's description grew. I then enquired what would be the smallest signs of getting back on track from her point of view and also, importantly, what the school would need to see to convince them 'that the Year 8 Christiana is here to stay'. This can sometimes be couched in terms of 'What are the minimum changes the school would need to see?'

The more we talked about Christiana in terms of her Year 8 self, the more her ideas blossomed. She really liked it when I asked her: 'What have you learnt from this Year 8 version that might be helpful now?' and she talked about knowing where the boundaries were and the fact that she was paying more attention to her studies. She was also reminded that she did have some good relationships with teachers. When asked what they liked about her, she talked about how she always had good ideas and that she also sometimes helped other students.

'It is important that descriptions are woven into ... relationships' (Ratner 2012: 98). Thus, through a description of the responses of others and the effect these responses may have, we can seek to widen the signs of difference or the domino effects of change, and we can look at the interactions that can best support these changes:

• *Asking students*: How will you know when people *do* notice the effort you are making and what difference would this make to you and what you do?
• *Asking staff*: How will students know when you have noticed a change in the way they are going about things? What might the student do in response? And if they did that, how might you respond?

This is not a script with stage directions for a play; the purpose is to create a sense of possibility where the 'Year 8 side' of all students can emerge, take shape and become part of the solution.

With the support of a mentor, Christiana managed the ups and downs of that term. Although never the 'perfect' student, she found ways to work within the confines of the school rules in a way that fitted with her desire to have fun and also do justice to her capacities academically. She talked about wanting to be a lawyer and I have to confess that, with her powers of argument, I would certainly want her on my side were I to be in court. There were also examples of when Christiana's natural leadership qualities were put to good use. During the Year 11 performance in which she had a major role, Christiana proved to be a great support to staff in motivating and keeping the rest of the cast on track. There was also the time I worked with a Year 8 student, Cal, when Christiana was in Year 9. Cal's report card was full of 'Achieved' comments across all three of his behaviour targets. When I enquired: 'How come?' Cal told me that Christiana had decided he needed taking in hand. So, every break and lunchtime, Cal would report to Christiana who would look at his report card. Whether through admiration or fear, it was extremely effective in keeping Cal's behaviour on track.

Part 8 Solution focus in Zanzibar: A case study

75. Stay open to differences!

Sometimes we encounter experiences in our working lives which stretch our thinking, our practice and our resilience. Between 2008 and 2010, I (YA) worked alongside my husband for the Ministry of Education in Zanzibar, Tanzania, as a volunteer for Voluntary Services Overseas (VSO). The task was to conduct a participatory research project into local perceptions of 'quality education and the school leadership needed to bring this about'. It was a daunting undertaking. However, it also provided the rare opportunity to work at an island-wide level from the local (teacher, class, school) to the global (the Ministry) and to explore how SF ideas and questions could be utilised to support those elements which are key in bringing about change whatever the context.

Zanzibar consists of a pair of wonderfully quirky islands full of colour, steeped in history and bustling with life. However, the challenges facing the education system in 2008 were immense. A rapid expansion of student numbers from 20,000 in 1964, 165,000 in 1997, to 285,000 in 2009 had occurred without the necessary infrastructure in terms of school buildings and teachers to support this. Local communities had to finance and build their own schools after which the Ministry would fund a roof and a teacher. Many schools ran double and even triple sessions in classrooms. Even so, a large class was only defined as such when there were more than 80 students, rising to 120 in subjects where there was a shortage of teachers, such as in maths and science. The majority of classrooms were sparsely furnished with no electricity or running water. Many students worked sitting on a concrete floor with few resources such as books or pens. I remember watching a group of children working and enquired why one boy was not writing. I was told he was waiting for his turn with the pencil. Teacher absenteeism was high and the percentage of students accessing higher education was almost negligible.

Our own living and working conditions also required some adjusting to, not least during a three month stretch when the entire island was without mains electricity. This affected our water supply, fan, fridge and use of our computer! Access to the internet involved a 5km bike ride to the nearest town. The absence of understanding about how systems worked often made it difficult to know how to proceed, who to refer to or what was acceptable. There was little in the way of equipment – precious flip chart paper was recycled and recycled. The 95% humidity was, at times, exhausting and access to rural schools was a time-consuming adventure.

However, broad descriptions and generalisations often mask the uniqueness of individuals and situations. Remaining open to differences that contained within them possibilities became an important thread throughout our work on the island. Although we needed to take account of the political, organisational and bureaucratic constraints, if we narrowed our views of what was possible, we would potentially narrow the options for all those with whom we worked.

Brief overview of the research project

We inherited a project framework which had already been agreed between VSO and the Commissioner for Education. It involved two phases: focus group discussions followed by individual interviews. Participants would be drawn from primary stakeholders (students, parents, teachers, head teachers) based in and around schools, secondary stakeholders (inspectors, local government officials, staff involved with teacher advancement) all directly linked with schools, and policy-making tertiary stakeholders at the Ministry level. The research methods and reporting style were part of a standard VSO staple which had been used across a number of different research projects worldwide.

76. Where do you position yourself and how do you get started?

In any piece of work there is a need to establish credibility in the eyes of the people we work with: trust and belief that we can 'do the job'. The expertise that SF offers is in the asking of particular kinds of questions that seek to elicit and centralise the ideas of the people we are working with. So the stance we took was one of curiosity: clarifying their visions, highlighting their successes and elaborating on the skills and expertise which had been important factors in supporting these.

Meeting with the directors

Good beginnings are pivotal in setting the tone for all that follows. Our first decision was to arrange a meeting with the Commissioner for Education and key Ministry officials (Directors). We began by enquiring about recent developments that the Directors were proud of. Even though there were a lot of concerns, this group of professionals had been working hard to build an effective education system. Finding out the 'what' and 'how' of successes was both validating of what they were doing and provided some clear indicators as to how initiatives were set up, carried out and supported. We heard about programmes at the Teacher Centres to further professional development, and how the Director for secondary education had been pioneering a system whereby new head teachers were interviewed for their posts and given guidance.

These current developments also represented an education system 'on the move'. Within this, the research could represent a part of a process that would potentially lead to more change rather than being viewed as an end in itself. In order to determine the most useful process, we sought to clarify two things: what information the research would reveal that would be different from what the Ministry already knew, and the hoped-for difference this information would make in supporting key developments. This was not easy because of the huge impact of limited funding and the difficulties this created. However, what was identified as an initial point of agreement was that *the critical element of quality education was the day-to-day, minute-by-minute processes in the classroom*. This gave us a starting point for our focus groups alongside the need to ensure that potential 'solution ideas' as well as concerns would be sought. In this way, the research gained definition in situ much as would be found in an action research model, and the meeting represented the start of an on-going dialogue with the Ministry in which we sought to remain close to their reality and hopes.

Working with the inspectorate

Our base was located within the inspectorate – a knowledgeable and influential group of 13 staff who visited schools, made suggestions and fed back to the Ministry. We sought their views on how change was initiated and rolled out, and were privileged to accompany them on their visits to schools. During each visit, we would similarly invite the head teachers into their own expertise about their schools and the changes they were seeking to instigate. At all times, we listened to the many concerns and at the same time began our search for the small shoots of success related to their future ideas. In this way, we also established credibility by building our knowledge of the island through the lens of the people who knew it best.

77. Data gathering phase

Focus groups

When faced with complex situations, there can be a danger in trying to tackle everything at once, with the subsequent effect of building a description so broad as to have little relevance to everyday situations. Taking the cue from our discussion with the Ministry, we decided to keep the focus group questions simple and directly related to on-the-ground realities of those experiencing and delivering quality education. Participants were asked to imagine they were walking into a classroom where there was such education happening and to describe what they would be seeing and hearing that would evidence this. They were additionally asked what would be happening *outside* the classroom, in the school and beyond, that would support what was happening *inside* the classroom. The aim was to provide a detailed picture at a micro level that could potentially inform policies at a macro level. The following sets of questions were vital in translating abstract or large concepts into concrete ideas and locating small yet significant details.

- *Actions*: What will be happening? What will you be doing? What will others be doing? What will (insert idea) look like?
- *Effects*: What difference will that make? What effect will that have?
- *Recognising existing good practice*: 'Which of these things are already happening?' also provides clues to more straightforward solutions.

Individual interviews

Questions for the individual interviews were directly influenced by the focus group findings, including issues such as encouraging student participation and enhancing the authority of head teachers. Exploring possible solutions to key challenges and looking for strengths helped to locate potential evidence that would support progress and change.

How do we respond when the answers so often pivot on the need for additional resources?

One of our biggest 'changamoto' ('challenges' in Kiswahili) was the overwhelming initial responses from participants about resources. This was entirely reasonable given the huge lack. However, it was unlikely that the volume of resources needed would be available in the near future. It is also often the case that resources do not per se lead to quality education. For example, at one school there was a shed full of unused wheelchairs; as the school was situated on a sandy beach, they were totally impractical. We were also shown a cupboard full of pristine science books which were considered to be so precious they were never opened. Without in any way negating the huge challenges, we needed to find a respectful way of moving beyond funding-related answers to help build a picture of quality education that realistically represented acceptance of the participants' viewpoints but not the limitations that were being attached.

The following proved to be the most useful in unearthing ideas that contained within them possibilities.

- Accepting the request and moving on, asking in an appropriate tone 'What else?' sometimes several times.
- Remaining open to the 'ideas behind an idea'. For example, when one participant suggested an aquarium as a sign of quality education, we had to park our thoughts of: 'How would an aquarium work in a classroom where there is no electricity?' and uncover the usefulness which often lurks behind such a statement. Pointing curiosity towards what *difference* an aquarium would make, led to a comment about the value of involving students in practical and concrete activities. This opened the way for exploring other signs of involving students in practical and concrete activities. The aquarium thus became a metaphor for a style and approach to education within which it might be just one part.
- Taking account of the wider context within which actions occur. For example, there were many complaints about teacher absenteeism. Further discussion revealed that teachers' wages were so low they were often forced to hold down two or more jobs. The act of finding this out in itself did not change the situation. However, it changed what we focused on and what we asked about. As we listened to what would be different in the future, alongside suggestions about an increase in wages, we also heard about other ideas related to improving the standing of teachers in the community, and one of the recommendation strands in our final report about raising the professional profile of teachers was born.

How do we maintain a non-judgemental stance?

There were points during the initial stages of the project when we were flagging under the weight of criticisms, judgements and difficulties that were being raised. At these times, it is very easy to start thinking in critical terms about the people we are working with. When our colleague Chris Iveson came to visit us with his family on holiday (lucky chap!), I complained to him about what was happening, in effect mirroring the criticism I was objecting to. In response he said: 'So, somehow it is about finding ways you can work in a culture that sees judgement and criticism as a way of supporting change?' Until this point I had been focusing on the seemingly impregnable barrier of judgement and criticism. By adding the phrase 'to support change' it transformed an opposition into an alignment around the core task of change – a shared common direction. Hearing comments within the context of desiring change rather than judgement made it easier to stand back and find those elements that could be most usefully explored.

78. Final meeting and report

Six themes emerged from our analysis of the key findings. These were discussed with the Ministry and formed the basis of the subsequent VSO house style report, Leading Learning (VSO International website). In doing so, we thought carefully about how to do justice to both the reality and the capacities for change.

- The themes, for example, head teacher authority and competence, co-ordinated training and planning, were deliberately broad and presented as a starting point with the space to re-shape and refine.
- We carefully considered the words we used. For example, describing the need to raise the professional profile of teachers rather than talking about the criticisms of unprofessionalism placed one foot already on the road to change; linking accountability with appreciation ensured that they both could make an appearance and afforded equal weighting to their potential value in promoting and supporting change.
- Possibly our most compelling intervention was the rigour with which we had searched out, in relation to each of the themes identified, examples of success and good practice already in view on the island. Providing a link between the wanted future and what was evident was a powerful affirmation of what was possible.

At the end of our presentation, the participants clapped and the Commissioner shook our hands, stating this was the research she had been hoping for. We later learnt that both were unprecedented occurrences. Staying close to the Commissioner's vision and that of her immediate colleagues meant that the report was signed off in record time and used to inform developments by the Ministry and the next phase of VSO interventions. Thus, the energy created was immediately utilised.

79. **What happened next?**

Having completed our assignment, there was a short time before we left the island during which we learnt about other shoots of development that were appearing. Many of these were small things in terms of actions and yet big things in terms of the thinking behind them. Creating a dialogue that helped people to focus on what was working rather than what wasn't was potentially one of the most sustainable legacies that we left. For example, the inspectorate included a section on their inspection form looking at what was working well and began to gather examples of good practice to share across the island.

Additionally, the director for secondary education asked us to help him design and roll out a coaching training programme for head teachers. One of the participants, who led a prestigious school in the capital Stonetown, had been so struck by the training that on returning to his school he immediately organised a session for all the staff. He also commented that he had begun to use the questions in discussions with students. He was joined by two other head teachers who were keen to develop coaching in their schools and the trio began to co-facilitate the groups with us, so that when we left, the programme could continue. We were privileged to observe these fledging trainers hone their own questioning skills as they took over the training.

80. **What did we learn?**

Framing questions in a way that people can relate to

SFP is about creating an experience that encourages changes and developments to grow organically. We would often open a session with an activity to facilitate participants in asking questions of each other. We chose those questions that we thought would sit most closely with, and be of most relevance to, our audience. For example, during a coaching training session, which was attended by representatives from the inspectorate, we placed alongside questions about the skills and ideas people brought to their work ('3 things you have been pleased to notice recently', '2 skills you bring to your work') a question about change which the participants viewed as an essential part of their roles ('1 thing you would like to be better at').

One of the inspectors subsequently described how she had used these questions with the rest of her team whilst waiting for a meeting to start. It had been great fun and they had found out many things about each other that they had not known before. For a tight knit group, who had worked together for years and were based in one room, this had been a very different experience. It also supported their focus on 'improvement'. A few months later, the same inspector reported that:

- thinking in this way had improved their observation skills as inspectors
- part of capacity building for teachers would now be to help them to look at their own skills and also to work alongside them to come up with their own ideas
- it had helped them to make things more individual rather than just looking at the larger problems.

'It's not what you look at, it is what you see'. (Henry Thoreau)

During our work on the island, we met with a wonderful head teacher of a rural school who, against the odds, was providing a rounded education for all the students in his care. When I returned to the island a year later, I found him in the process of building a library. I was able to give a donation from money raised by a sponsored swim my son had undertaken to help with the next stages of providing a secure door and windows. That evening, I spoke with the current VSO volunteer who was working in the school. I was soundly berated for my naivety in handing over money to a head teacher he felt was secretive and untrustworthy; *'He never meets without first asking what we will be discussing. I think he has things to hide. Well, that is the last you will see of that money. I doubt he will mention it to me'.*

The following day, to the volunteer's credit, I received an apology. On visiting the school, he had been greeted by the head teacher brimming with excitement about the donation and was shown detailed plans about how the money would be used. The volunteer reported that he had now seen the head teacher in a completely different light, as someone who was organised and considered in the way he went about things, committed to his school and who wanted to make the most of any opportunity.

We need to be clear at all times about what we are doing and why

A few months into my time on Zanzibar I was asked to immediately present myself to the Chief of Police for an unspecified reason. As I entered his office, filled with trepidation, I was asked several questions about my name and my reason for being on the island. The Chief of Police then asked: 'What do you think of my English?' I had no idea where this was heading but thought a compliment was the most prudent response. He followed this up with a further enquiry about whether his English needed improving. I sat there desperately trying to figure out why he was asking me these questions. I began to think: 'If I am charged with something who can I call on or rely on?' I scrabbled around for the 'right' answer and in the end mumbled some platitude about how we are all lifelong learners, and then held my breath. Finally, after several more minutes, the nub of the conversation was revealed: Would I bring him some books to help with his English? Sure! I left after 20 minutes of sweat-inducing anxiety, via the finger printing section, to return post haste with as many books as I could carry.

It left a huge impression on me about the need to create a space of safety in which the views of the people we are working with can be sought and expressed. This safety can be in part created by the transparency with which we ask questions and also a shared understanding of the purpose of the conversation. It also made me consider the support options which many of the people we work with might not have knowledge about, or access to.

Did we do enough?

Our work on Zanzibar felt, at times, like a drop in the ocean and I left feeling that there was so much more we could have done. When faced with situations of huge complexity or overwhelming odds, it is easy to question or undermine what you are doing. At these times, it is good to remember that even one small change somewhere can make a difference, and so it seems apt to end with a street seller named Saidi who had left school at 14. In the early days, he helped us to find our son who we thought had gone missing (it turned out he had gone to the post office to try and use the internet!) and through this a friendship developed which lasted during our time on the island and beyond. We swapped English and Kiswahili lessons. We helped Saidi to capitalise on his selling skills to build a more profitable business and linked him with a short-term VSO volunteer from Deloittes. When he contracted malaria, we took Saidi food and he spent time acquainting us with many aspects of Zanzibar life that we would not have experienced. At our final meeting, he produced from his pocket a huge wad of bank notes that he had saved, saying that we had changed his life by believing in him and helping him to build his business. He now wanted to go back to school to learn to read and write. When I returned a year later, I set up some writing and reading lessons for him with a volunteer from the Philippines. The following year, I received a handwritten postcard from Saidi saying that he was leaving Zanzibar and returning to mainland Tanzania where he was originally from. Having bought a property on Zanzibar, he was now selling it, which would provide him with capital for the next stage of his journey.

Kiswahili proverbs

Alongside our reworking of a Kiswahili proverb: 'It is only the wearer of the shoe who knows where it pinches' into: 'It is only the wearer of the shoe who knows where it is comfortable', we added one of our own: 'If you try and conduct a focus group in a hut with a corrugated iron roof in a torrential downpour, you are unlikely to hear the responses'.

Final thoughts

We are very rarely faced with the perfect situation or resources, but we can create opportunities to bring out the best in the people we are working with. SFP offered me a clear and optimistic framework that kept me searching, trying and believing.

Acknowledgment

As the foregoing account shows, during our time on Zanzibar we met many people we felt privileged to get to know and who we will never forget. And above all we are grateful to VSO for the vital work they do and for giving us the opportunity to fulfil the dream of a lifetime.

Index

Printed in Great Britain
by Amazon

37421903R00086